21st Century Management
A personal blog

Moria Levy

ROM Knowledgeware

Published by ROM Knowledgeware, Inc., Tel-Aviv, Israel

Published simultaneously in USA.

Designed by Or Levy

For more information please visit our website at www.kmrom.com/english, or call 972-77-5020-771.

Library of Congress Cataloging-in-Publication Data:

Levy, Moria

21st Century Management: A personal blog

ISBN 13: 978-1453719220

To my Dear family

Contents

Why Blogging? Why me?

Hello. I would like to introduce myself. My name is Moria Levy, I am 43 years old, and I am the founder and manager of ROM Knowledgeware, an Israeli Knowledge Management firm I founded nine years ago. I also have a husband (Ran), four children (Or, Sapir, Tomer and Kfir), a dog and a parrot.

I write a lot, mostly in the Hebrew KM magazine "2know." I have been writing for many years (nearly a decade). I write about what I do - Knowledge Management. Until now I wrote as I was educated at university. My writing focused on Knowledge Management methodologies and was meant for professionals dealing with KM. As I wrote in Hebrew, this meant addressing a unique group of a few thousand people. My writing never referred to me. I maintained a distance keeping "Moria," the person, behind. That, I was taught, is dignified writing. The writer is of no interest; only the writing is important.

Last year I felt a change. One can find much personal writing on the net. This trend started earlier, but since 2007 it has spread rapidly. As in other disciplines, we have come to understand that connecting the rational and the emotional has unique potential. It enables synergy. Writing in a personal style gives every person the ability to better express his or herself and thereby to better express thoughts and ideas. The bottom line: this from-the-heart style of writing often yields good quality.

This blog will be focused on management; Management in an era of knowledge. The 21st century is characterized as a knowledge century, and we are knowledge workers: knowledge is a central component in workers' occupation and success. The first to develop this perception of knowledge workers and their management was Peter Drucker. I will not elaborate here on his ideas, as this is beyond the scope of this post.

As managers, we need to act differently than we did in a world where knowledge was less central. Knowledge is so important today that it affects all aspects of work and management: we must take it into account when we hire people (how to choose the right employees when existing knowledge is so important, when sharing and expanding it in the organization is critical); we must consider it when we think about workers' development, cultivation and retention;. we must take it into consideration when analyzing our core competencies (yes, we are one small global village); we must take it into consideration when we think about our customers relations (think about a patient coming to a physician having specific knowledge and recommended treatment, downloaded from the Internet, of which the MD is unaware!); and we must take it into account when we analyze our competitors (understanding that it is so easy for them to know what we know and what guides us in our activities).

When I blog, I express three aspects of myself:
First, Me as a manager, dealing, like many of you, with strategic planning, personnel, financing, customer relations and so on;
Second, Me as a Knowledge Management expert: aware of the needs, the possible solutions, but also of the difficulty in implementing these solutions in real life organizations.
And finally, Me as a person, with the values I was brought up with and with the principles I crystallized over the years, which have made me into the person I am today.
I hope the readers will find this blog interesting and helpful in thinking about and dealing with management in the knowledge era.
I hope to receive your comments and to learn from them. Internet talkbacks give us an additional layer and enrich the readers as well as the writer.
I will also be glad to read your ideas about knowledge management issues that you would like to see in this blog.
It takes time for a good blog to establish its position. I thank you in advance for your trust and patience.

Yours,

    Moria

 Roni Klinsky, 10/20/07, 11:24

The blog might be an excellent channel for sharing such knowledge with managers. Good Luck!

Linda, 08/11/08, 19:03

Hello, Moria. Your site was made known to me. Much of what is written seems connected to organizational life and not to Olympus. Thanks, Linda

Anonymous, 04/07/09, 06:29

Your blog is one of many I have read, but it is the only one I read to the end.

2007-10-11 10:27

 # Who is the worker we manage?

Twenty years ago, during my military service. I was put in command of a group of ten computer professionals. I wasn't trained in managing people, yet I believe I did a fair job. Today I manage people and I feel as if it is a different story altogether - a different type of management. I have come to agree with the saying that having 10 employees is not 1 times managing 10 but 10 times managing 1. Every person has to be managed differently; every employee needs to be spoken to and listened to in a unique way. It took me several years to understand that the way I manage my employees is as important as developing the KM discipline (my profession). What has changed?

At first, I thought it was me. Over the years, I have matured; some would say I grew older. This is true, of course. My perspective on life is different now than it was. I do not, however, think that this explains it all. Workers in the 21st century are not the workers of 20 years ago. Industry is changing. These workers, which Drucker called knowledge workers, act and develop differently from the production line workers that were so typical of the 20th century.

In this post, I shall try to define the knowledge workers' profile. How did I learn who they are and how to work with them? I was helped partly by experience, partly by intuition, and largely by reading (on this issue, mainly Drucker's books). There are some things I still do not know. Like many others I also make mistakes. I err and try to improve myself; sometimes successfully, other times less so.

The knowledge worker is an independent worker. S/he makes most decisions alone, first and foremost deciding every day whether or not to continue working in the same place. If in the past people came to work to earn their living and were dependent on the organization, today we are in a very different situation. Salary is not enough for the knowledge worker. Do not misunderstand me: they indeed earn a nice salary. Nevertheless, the knowledge worker is looking for more: professional satisfaction, a nurturing environment and future possibilities (see Herzberg's theory on hygiene). Drucker states that we have to treat our knowledge workers as volunteers. We have to convince them, almost on a daily basis, to continue working voluntarily with us. This is definitely not an easy task and one that we would be happy to reject, That choice though is probably not ours.

What else can be said about knowledge workers?
A knowledge worker needs a lot information and knowledge in order to perform his/her job. This, of course, is not surprising since s/he is termed "knowledge worker." Yet it should be clear that the information and knowledge are not static. What characterizes the knowledge worker is that his knowledge is developing constantly and not just from doing his/her job. We must leave time for the knowledge worker to read and learn: from professional magazines and books, from surfing the internet and from attending conferences and inter-organizational meetings. A knowledge worker who does not develop his/her skills will eventually experience difficulties in achieving success. I must confess that even 5-6 years ago I tried to maximize the business working hours for all of my employees. Later on, I learned to include professional training on a monthly basis. Today I know that this also is not enough. Now I encourage my people to write articles, as working on an article includes, in addition to the writing itself, a lot of reading, analyzing, arranging thoughts and building a concept. I doubled the training hours, including other types of learning in addition to lectures. And all of this is probably still inadequate. Is this only because I deal with an innovative developing profession (Knowledge Management)? This is only partly correct. All around me I see my customers dealing with developing professions and innovative aspects: hardware engineers are dealing more and more with software and integration; pharmaceutical researchers are constantly

developing chemistry expertise and knowledge of biology, genetics etc. Insurance agents, who used to offer me exactly what they were told to offer by their insurance companies, today work with many insurance companies, offering different types of life insurance, loans, health insurance and other financial products; they all work with various companies and offer me the best fit (for me or for them). One of my customers, dealing with child fostering, spends important time learning the models of fostering that work best in other countries. I can go on providing many more examples from various professional disciplines. The message is clear: workers are knowledge workers and those who do not develop constantly, no matter how experienced, will find it hard to continue progressing. Without relying on existing wide knowledge, developing the new knowledge and achieving future success is in jeopardy.

An interesting fact, derived from the above, is that the knowledge worker knows, for his/ her specific tasks, more than the manager in-charge. Even if managers come from the same professional discipline, they cannot be experts in all the sub-expertise under their responsibility. There will always be some field in which they have no experience; there will always be the problem that their knowledge is outdated. As is well known, the world is fast evolving. This poses a challenging situation. Most of us managers, until today, based our authority on professionalism. Personally, I can say that I have learned from experience and that I actually understand knowledge management methodologies (my professional expertise), having studied math and computers at university. I lack the knowledge of my employees who learned industrial engineering or organizational behavior. I lack the knowledge that my employees developed yesterday and the day before, while I was busy managing the company.

The knowledge worker is autonomous. Even though surrounded by teams, each one has to specialize in specific tasks, collecting, filtering, analyzing and deciding according to the information and knowledge gathered. Nevertheless, the knowledge worker has to know how to share - not only decisions but also information and knowledge that can help others better perform their job. Sharing, and even teaching, is part of the knowledge-working job. It helps others and it helps the knowledge worker, who better understands his/her knowledge after discussing it with those who were taught. As the famous Jewish saying goes: "I have learned from all my teachers; however, I have learned the most from my pupils".

Knowledge workers manage their own time; they make their own decisions; they multi task much more than in the past.

Knowledge workers are self-managers, and we thus find ourselves managing managers.
This of course changes the way we ought to manage.

Is this all good? I believe it is, and not only because we do not have any other choice but to adapt. I believe that we, as managers, develop personally from this challenge of managing knowledge workers. I can say for myself that I do.

And I know that when I succeed, the satisfaction is enormous. So, yes, I also benefit.
Tired but satisfied (and now you know why).

Yours,
    Moria

dr Jimmy, 10/18/2007, 16:33

Moria, kudos on the blog. Continue to remove yourself from academic writing, maybe in a column that is a kind of personal diary organizing your thoughts in the field. Remember that most of the people who will read your forum know the terms, so you don't need to expand. In other words, write from the heart. Lots of luck. I hope you will contribute.

Yaniv, 10/19/2007, 10:23

Maybe the majority of your readers will not request expansion, but a minority, including me, will. For example, I still do not quite understand what a knowledge manager deals with and what his role is. Isn't the one who operates the systems an industrial and managerial engineer? What role remains for the knowledge manager (the information specialist that studied so hard at Bar Ilan University)?

Anyway, it is pleasant to read your writing. One really feels that your company has understood that times have changed (the photos and phone numbers of your workers show your openness). You have nothing to hide – that is simply wonderful.

Roni Klinski, 10/20/2007, 11:33

I agree with the principles that you present, but the mechanisms for appropriate knowledge workers to flourish are lacking. By the way, it comes across in the writing that all the workers in an organization are knowledge workers on the same level. Clearly, this is not the case. Is there a study that deals with the differences between the levels and between the types of tasks (research, marketing, finance etc)?

Hiring employees

Hiring people, like many other management activities, is not a new task. We read many articles discussing the issue; as markets expand, companies are doing a lot of hiring.

In my firm, the hiring process has become complicated. This happens despite my pragmatic nature and my tendency to avoid bureaucracy. Why is this happening? Like everyone else, I am afraid of a hiring process that is not successful enough. First, I see the employee that may be asked to leave. Laying off an employee is always a very unpleasant situation. Companies should not keep people who do not fit in, but we always have to do everything we can to avoid removing and replacing people. I believe that every time we fire someone we leave a scar in his or her heart. I admit that I have fired several people in the past, but when I do so, I try to leave the employee with their dignity. And I try to learn a lesson from each episode, in order to reduce the chances of finding myself again in a similar situation.

Beside the personal discomfort, firing people in order to replace them with others is a business loss. It is also a personal loss for those left in the organization. We encourage our employees to develop informal relationships with one another. Some of us (like me) call it "family values;" others use different terms. Good interrelations develop into good working environments and trust. Trust enables sharing and knowledge development. Besides, it gives each one of us a good feeling when we enter the office each morning.

The bottom line: We hire not to fire. Very simple indeed. So what is there to write about? And what is new from a knowledge perspective?

Looking at this issue from a knowledge perspective gives us some insights:
in a knowledge era, a worker has much to learn during his or her stay in the organization. Sometimes, the knowledge gained in those years of work is more important than the knowledge s/he had when hired. In this respect, a candidate's ability and desire to learn are more important than their professional CV.
In the knowledge era, it is important not only to know, but also to be able to teach others and to learn from them. It is not enough to learn from books and from the Internet. A candidate's ability to work with others, to teach and learn from them is an important election parameter.

In the knowledge era, workers choose the place in which they work no less than the organization chooses them. Adequacy between the organization's values (the real ones, not those posted on the office walls) and the worker's personal values will contribute to the worker's success in the company. We have to remember that people do not remain in jobs for money only. There will always be someone somewhere else that will offer more. Employees want to feel that they are achieving their goals and working the "right" way. Organizations must have the same feeling regarding their employees: the managers must feel that each employee is part of the progress of the whole. A personal conversation with the candidate may be the way to test the adequacy: a conversation about goals and wishes, about what the employee enjoys doing in his or her free time and what makes him/her them happy. Such a conversation should not be held by the HR department. Organizations are built from smaller groups, each with its sub-values and ways of doing things. A conversation held with HR seems too theoretical. It is better that the manager of the group holds such a conversation and personally makes such a decision. Yes, there are other points that can help, but I have tried to list the major ones: learning ability, sharing ability and value adequacy.

Have I fallen when hiring people? I sure have. But, I have improved. And

I'm still working on it. I would appreciate hearing from your experience too, especially from the knowledge perspective.

Yours,
Moria

 Alon Sarar, 11/15/2007, 17:05

Hello Moria,

I was pleased to see the respectful approach you present here and its immediate translation into action. I want to suggest going a step further, or actually highlighting an assumption hidden in your words. You present a very responsible approach towards the worker, but do not talk enough about how you demand responsibility from him/her, something, I understand from your words, in which you are interested. In a (small) number of interviews in which I participated when I was a hired employee, the interviewers gradually placed me in the work situation. They described the work to me and together we defined the challenges and deliverables, describing the future personal growth that should take place while filling the position.

This kind of interview made me firstly understand what I was getting into, and whether or not I wanted the position and its challenges. At the same time, I took responsibility also for my own learning and for the way in which I was supposed to contribute to the learning of the organization, whether with knowledge I already had, or with knowledge I was expected to acquire by theory or action.

This taking of responsibility is an important step in establishing a position of seeing eye to eye and in the obligation to push forward the personal contribution to the organization's knowledge, as part of the expectations of the position.

When the worker also knows to say a few words on the issue on his initiative, apparently he has really considered the position and knows what he is getting into. Through his initiated words, one may evaluate

16

how much the worker and the demands, responsibility and learning fit each other.

Simon, 11/20/2007, 11:35

Moria,

I especially liked the dimension of values adequacy. I have seen serious failures on exactly this issue, which is often neglected and not adequately considered. Your suggestion to have a personal conversation, in which the worker's values and real opinions are revealed, is an important one that I have been implementing already for many years.

I too have fallen in worker recruitment, but relatively little and more importantly, I have improved.

A considerable percentage of the managers working today in different engineering companies are people that I personally recruited.

New employee incorporation

Recently, one of my employees left the organization. The hiring process was successful. He fit. He contributed to the company and benefited from it. He left because he received a better opportunity elsewhere, an opportunity to become a manager.

I am sorry and a bit sad. He could have developed and achieved professional success in our company. But life continues. We will go on evolving with others.

I could have let go and said that there will always be better opportunities, no matter what we give or do. That is correct. But one must not stop there. That is an easy way out. Every process of changing the workplace includes two phases: A phase of leaving the old and a phase of starting anew.

No doubt, that leaving us, in this situation, was a result of not a sufficiently fine process of new employee incorporation. You may ask how long this employee worked in the company. Indeed, this is a fair question. He was with us nine months. So long? How long does it take to absorb someone new and teach him or her the job?

This is the topic I want to discuss and share: new employee incorporation.

Hiring a knowledge worker and teaching the job takes a year, at least.
Why? Because today most jobs differ from organization to organization. Think about the knowledge workers in your organization, or even better, think about yourself. Try to remember what you did before, and before that, and how different that all was from your current position. This is the knowledge era: work processes are roughly defined; the knowledge toolbox, with professional, organizational and market defined aspects, makes the job what it is. And these change rapidly.

All this is why employment incorporation takes time. This is why it is not a trivial process.

The best way to learn, as studies have discovered, is by experience. But this process is expensive, risky and not satisfactory by itself. It is expensive, because if performed in a radical way, does not consider existing knowledge; it is risky, because of the performance results in the apprenticeship period; and it is not satisfactory by itself as different people learn differently. Every person needs a different mix of: learning from ideas and concepts, learning from case studies, learning from observing others (reflection) and learning by doing (See Kolb: "Experience as the source of Learning and Development").

A new employee must be taught by both general unified training, with which we start, and personal training, which becomes more significant later on. The general training provides the essential foundations of knowledge necessary for better job understanding. The personal training fills in the specific voids, but more importantly, is tailored to the learning style of the person to be trained.

Some points to emphasize:

a. Expectations of the new employee have to be adjusted, so that s/he understands that it takes at least a year until the job is understood thoroughly and s/he can move forward.

b. The manager's responsibility is to analyze what the worker does not know that he does not know (this is the tricky type of knowledge). This is not a one time analysis, rather a routine. Practically, it is recommended to set training meetings in which, through open conversation, professional topics are discussed and tackled.

c. Stepwise loading of tasks. The sooner we appoint diverse tasks, the more time it will take to adjust. Tasks? Yes. Loading? All right. But diverse? This needs to be stepwise or else the new employee incorporation process will turn out to be longer. This may sound trivial, but if we define a year long process, it is less trivial.

And the last tip is maybe the most important: there are no shortcuts. I knew about all the points above, and usually, that is the way I manage. Yet I made a mistake. I forgot (or chose to forget) that there are no exceptions and no shortcuts.

I paid the price.

Yours,
    Moria

Aharon R., 11/15/2007, 16:50
The article is excellent and it illustrates what is happening today in many organizations in which there is a large turnover, resulting in a loss of knowledge and in some instances the creation of new and erroneous information that in turn becomes erroneous knowledge.
The contempt for the human resource shown in saying that "each person has his/her replacement that is cheaper" only ends up harming the organization.

Alon Sherer, 11/17/2007, 22:32
I feel as if you are only hitting the tip of the iceberg. Professionalism, the way I see it, is a process founded on personal standards, on one hand, and on the construction of knowledge, on the other. You speak about the initial absorption as a one year process, but one who really invests, as you mentioned, in constant personal tutelage, really builds bodies of knowledge. Often one knowledge worker must hold several bodies of knowledge, and must also know how to integrate them in order to really be good. Even when this construction is carried out and the worker feels that he is progressing professionally, sometimes the temptation for a position or a better salary in a different place will tip the scales.

It is painful. It is frustrating because really, as Aharon mentioned, there are few places that offer the opportunity to really, thoroughly and systematically develop.

I personally think that workers should see a more nurtured inner circle and should desire to be part of it. They also need to go through quite a significant trial period before one starts to really invest in them. It is really a relationship.

Ron, 11/15/09, 02:11

It is absolutely true that whenever an employer sets aside an employee - there is some or more sadness in the air.

However, let's not forget that whenever an employee resigns that might be as painful to the employer as to the employee - especially in small structured firms. Well done.

Ron Smuha

Thoughts regarding Knowledge Management

For those who do not know me, I have been working, living and breathing Knowledge Management for the past nine years. Knowledge Management is not the same as managing knowledge workers. It deals with preserving, sharing and creating the organizational knowledge, using well-defined methodologies and focusing on organizational business needs.

A week ago, I met a colleague that was in the KM industry for many years and left. He is busy nowadays in some very different area - the entertainment e-business. The truth is that I was surprised. This person was one of the first people in Israel that dealt with Knowledge Management, and he ran a successful company in this field. His PhD was about knowledge maps. I was even more surprised by the speech he gave me a few minutes later.

"You are brave," he said, "Knowledge Management will fail as a discipline." On the one hand, he flattered me for having the strength / the will / the innocence to continue with Knowledge Management. He was very happy to hear that I am working on my PhD. in Knowledge Management. On the other hand, he recommended that I leave this field and find something else in which to make my living.

"Why leave?" I asked. "The Knowledge Management discipline," he explained, "is in contrast to human nature. People are not willing to share. Organizations are afraid, especially from the power that comes with managing KM. Most organizations that started large Knowledge Management projects," he added, "stopped after two or three years, in many cases firing the CKO's who led the process." I started running scenes from the past years in my head. Yes, there were several organizations that did not continue; and yes, there were CKO's that left their jobs, and not always in the best of circumstances.

There was something to what he was saying. Too many times I remembered Knowledge Management projects ending because of problems and struggles between people. However, the more I thought about it, the more I realized that in all cases KM was the victim, not the trigger, of these struggles. Once, there was the CEO who believed in KM (and some other great ideas) but did not believe that he had to communicate any of his ideas to the managers who were supposed to actually share. The day he left, and one of these managers replaced him, all the good ideas, including KM, were cancelled. In a different case, the CEO worked directly with the KM activities manager, although there was a manager in between (the boss of the latter). The intermediate manager was not part of the process. At the first chance he had, after the CEO was replaced, he cut off the budget. Unfortunately there are more examples and, at least in both of the organizations I refer to, there were already success stories and benefits resulting from Knowledge Management activities.

"Isn't knowledge an important asset, critical for organizations' success?" I asked this colleague. "Very important," he answered. "That is why there are so many struggles around the issue. So why stay?"

I left worried and troubled. Am I just stubborn? Maybe it is just hard to recognize truth when one is so deeply involved?

I find myself since thinking about the issue a lot. I do believe in people; I want to believe in them. I believe in organizations, and I believe that if Knowledge is an important asset, even critical, organizations should manage it, and even positively. It must happen, because it is right that it should. It is not enough to find ways to manage the knowledge workers. Knowledge itself must be managed. The two are interconnected and, of course, there are overlaps. However, these are two defined disciplines: Management and Knowledge Management.

I have learned a lesson here regarding the management of knowledge workers. Many of the ideas these workers will suggest will not be trivial. Precisely these innovative, non-trivial, ideas will be the ones most difficult for the organization to accept. There will be those in favor, but probably more people would reject them. People and organizations are afraid of replacing the old with the new. People are terrified when a good idea comes from someone else, and they try to reject it. Many times an idea is rejected until it is proven - and sometimes even after. Our job, as managers, is to enable: not only the idea itself and its progress on the practical level, but also its acceptance by people. And that is not easy.

I hope I did not leave you with a melancholy impression. I promise some happy and smiley posts in the future. I promise, for those wondering, that I am not leaving Knowledge Management. Not now. Too much has yet to be done.

Yours,
Moria

 Anatoly Yudochsky, 12/02/2007, 10:09
I want to relate to the words of the respected doctor who left the field with the following explanation: "The Knowledge Management discipline," he explained, "is in contrast to human nature. People are not willing to share. Organizations are afraid to share information ..." It can't be sweepingly stated that people do not want to share their knowledge. Most people really want and even like to share knowledge, since it gives them a sense that what they have done is an accomplishment; it's important and someone, other than themselves, needs it. This is indeed a part of human nature. Various schools (professional, art, music, etc.) have come about in this way. Another example is a dynasty – when knowledge of a specific skill is transferred to

the next generation of the family (or not), which can appreciate it and continue the dynasty.

The situation is very different in organizations. This is because of the feeling that most staff members have of "temporary work." Even if a person comes to work for many years, it's rare that he will remain in one organization all his life. Employees usually aim to integrate into the organization and move forward professionally and personally. It is very rare that their aim is to contribute knowledge to the organization and create a new tradition as part of the corporate culture.

This means that the organization's knowledge manager has to find reasons for workers to share information, providing them with something important to them personally over and above the recognition from management that supports information sharing.

You were correct in saying that knowledge management is a change that should transform organizational culture and ultimately industrial culture. Obviously this will not happen quickly, so please do not give up mid way :)

Alon Sherer, 12/03/2007, 16:48

One of the troubles growing out of MBO, or at least one of the critiques, is that people do what is managed as a tasks. Knowledge, like other intangible assets, is still not defined as a task, Managers who report to boards of directors, and sometimes even company owners, find it difficult to manage a resource that has only an invisible yield.

However, there are always those who have faith that promote pioneering social phenomena. This phenomenon has also pioneers and is, in my opinion, on the verge of becoming fashionable. So, I guess it will become a part of management headquarters, similar to Human Resources. Today the function is obvious, although we cannot take for granted using it wisely.

These two areas are like the bass in a jazz ensemble – you can do without it, but it will never be the same thing

Simon, 12/16/2007, 17:06

Moria,

Well done on your courage to speak with such great clarity and openness in your blog "Reflections on Knowledge Management." I also find myself quite often thrashing about these same questions (and having less courage to ask them out loud):

Are we not trying to do something that is against human nature? Are we too naive about the INCENTIVE SYSTEM that motivates people to share knowledge?

I have complete faith in one thing: every employee (actually every person) has an inner urge to be the best he can possibly be at work, family and in every domain in which he operates. Is it possible to deduce that he will use any means to satisfy this urge, including "even" sharing his knowledge with others? In my opinion the answer is complex.

People act on and are driven by interests (INCENTIVE). One of the most powerful mechanisms is the comparison to others. If a person thinks he might gain an advantage over others by preserving his unique knowledge possessed - he will not share.

This might be even more true in this era of free access to knowledge. Today with just a few clicks you can get access to information and knowledge that once you could only dream about. Take for example a situation where a sick person (God forbid) can ask tough questions of a doctor (even an expert) just because of his ability to gain relevant information about the disease from which he suffers. In the past it would have been unthinkable to argue with a doctor ...

Therefore, paradoxically, the more the access to knowledge increases, the higher its "price" become, and perhaps, as a result, people who have a very specific type of knowledge will want to keep it to themselves.

I do not feel that I have solved the problem; it is certainly worth more profound thought. ...

Simon

Ronit Nechemia, 02/29/2008, 17:58

I think like you, Moria.

Our hope is not lost.

I'm too have been trying to implant a culture of knowledge management in a segment of the population that is considered very difficult when it comes to sharing knowledge and information – Israeli teachers.

I try to encourage them that sharing materials saves time and effort and that there is no need to invent the wheel each time over. I hope and recommend that you follow the process in my blog: "Knowledge Management – A Path and Value"

Pelpal, 03/11/2009 18:15

Eating meat is also contrary to human nature, and so are many other things, but they still happen. I am in the planned learning field, and I believe that the Y- Generation will present new challenges to this field, when most learning in procedural and declarative knowledge is dissolving in favor of concepts, mechanisms, tools and knowledge management in general.

So there is a future. At least in my opinion.

Working from home

Working from home. This is a capability that is born thanks to technology, but no less thanks to many of us being knowledge workers. Production workers, even having access to the wonderful technologies of Internet, laptops, Emails and cellular telephones, will never be able to work from home. Also some knowledge workers cannot, at least for some of the time, work from home. Appointments with customers and meetings at the office are part of the tasks better performed not in the home. Yet it is obvious that we have advanced relative to a decade ago.

I will state in advance that I'm not speaking about full time work from home. This is possible sometimes, and is more common in some places around the world, but this is not the subject of this post. Here I write about working in an office and/or with customers, but occasionally combining working from home

Why should one enable working from home?
For many reasons. First, it saves the worker or the organization travel costs. More importantly, however, it saves time. For most of us who do not live next to the office, time saved can amount to two or three hours a day. This is significant relative to our free non-sleeping hours. We live in an era where life and work are mixed and almost blended. We receive private calls on work time. We get and send SMSs during meetings, trying to see what is happening back at home, like why the pizza we ordered for the kids did not arrive on time. At home, we continue to receive calls from work, and mainly, to write and receive emails, often until the late hours of night. Those of you who dream of cutting these relations and imitating the way our parents used to work will probably be disappointed. Work-life-balance experts say that the levels can be reduced; it is recommended to turn off the phone and computer when

28

having guests, going to parties or to the movies. But to truly reverse the situation is probably impossible. What we can do is compensate; we can enable technology that brought all this to work in our favor as well: we can encourage our employees to work more flexible hours, so they can take their kids from kindergarten or school and continue working later on; we can enable our employees to arrive a bit later, after rush hour and start the first hour from home; we can enable them to work, one day a week, from home.

Working from home gives us much more than savings in time. The organization benefits, on some level, from operational savings. In most cases, work done at home is more effective, compared to the same work done in the office. However, the main benefit is in the change of spirit and the good feeling of the employee. I personally take a day off, from time to time, and work from home. When I see that the day I planned to work from home is near, and was not yet cancelled by some urgent last minute meeting, I feel happy. On regular days I wear suits to the office. On days I work at home, I always wear jeans, deliberately, as part of creating the right atmosphere.

When is work from home applicable?
The first condition is, of course, that there is back office work that can be performed at home. This is the type of work that requires no specific software unreachable from home, no tight interaction with colleagues or meetings with customers etc. It is not wise to work at home and speak all day on the phone with the office or the customer.

No less important is the responsibility of the employee working from home: not to stay in pyjamas; not to peek at TV; not to go in and out of the kitchen 20 times a day; to know to say no to the children who do not understand how is it that mom or dad is working and unavailable, even though s/he is home.

Knowledge workers are highly independent employees. Therefore, it is reasonable to assume that they will have work that can be done outside the office, and without colleagues. It is also assumed that they have the responsibility required for working from home.

What is the manager's job?
The manager should not automatically enable working from home to all employees under all conditions. The manager has to first clarify the responsibility required and check if each employee indeed can work from home effectively.
The manager's responsibility (or this can be defined organizationally) is to decide how frequently to enable work from home (once a week, once in two weeks, or once a month).
The manager's job is to supervise the work from home, to see that the employee does not postpone important tasks just to be at home, and to see that the employee indeed knows how to work from home effectively.

By enabling working from home, we tell our employees, in one more way: we trust you!
Working from home is beneficial for the employee, and not less so, for organizations.

Your opinions are welcomed.

Yours,
    Moria

Anonymous, 08/13/2009, 13:12

Brilliant article! A correct and excellent article.

Ayal, 10/05/2009, 01:03

A successful article. Definitely covers the topic and all its aspects.

Anonymous, 10/18/2009, 15:12

Well done for this article!, You definitely cover the whole foundation for work from home.

 # Trust

A week ago, mid-week, I went on vacation with my husband to a ski-school. Do not misunderstand me; I did not travel to Switzerland or some other pastoral locale you may imagine, just to a big hall, filled with some large simulators, in Herzelia, near Tel Aviv, in Israel. To those interested in the idea, this is probably a useful way to for non-skiers to practice ski skills, enabling the trip to the real ski sites to be as enjoyable as possible. However, this is not the topic I wish to share in today's post. I will only add, before continuing, that I am not much of an athlete, and when I once did try to ski (really ski, on a mountain in Switzerland), it was not as easy as I would have wished. Well, this time I found myself, twenty minutes into the lesson, holding the instructor with both my hands, begging her not to let go. This young woman was a complete stranger just half an hour before. And there I found myself putting my faith in her, and trusting her more than I trust people whom I know for months and years.

Trust. Trust is something that usually is built up after a long period, after some acquaintance. It is true that in extreme cases (and fear) this period may be shortened. This is a common technique used in various workshops. However, here in this post, I wish to speak about the process: the process of building trust.

Trust is a significant element in the knowledge workers' toolbox, helping them to perform their job. All Knowledge Management philosophers have spoke about trust and its influence on our willingness to share knowledge. I have written, in one of the first posts, about the importance of knowledge sharing to the success of knowledge workers. Trust, of course, is a significant element aiding the performance of all workers, even those who stand in the production line and feed in materials. Nevertheless, the significance of trust grows in the case of knowledge workers. For them, the motivation and integration with other employees are key factors for success.

As we understand, building trust, or more precisely nurturing it, is not that simple. We are speaking about a complicated and very sensitive process, which is hard to build, and too easy to destroy. The process becomes even more complicated as the manager has to nurture three separate zones of trust with respect to the knowledge workers s/he is in charge of.

First, trust must be built so that employees believe and trust the manager and the organization. Nurturing values such as truthfulness, honesty and organizational transparency can be a practical way to build trust; minimizing the gap between our words and our actions and being honest, not only to employees but also to customers and competitors, aid in creating trust between employee, management and the organization. I believe that the best way to bring employees to trust me is to trust them.

Trust, however, should not only be aimed at the manager and organization. The manager has to nurture an atmosphere of trust between the employees. Tools that can help here are diverse: encouraging shared activities after work hours, or activities unrelated to the job (trips, eating together, etc.); building cellular billing programs so that conversations between employees are free or very cheap; informing employees when their colleagues are missing from work, wherever possible, causing them to take an interest in one another; reminding employees of birthdays; making professional successes public; running events with families etc. The trust is built in ever growing circles, where the most important circle is the close one, where frequent interfaces take place. It must be noted that this is the easiest circle of trust to nurture as people hold face-to-face meetings.

The last zone of trust is with the customers. As already written above regarding trust of managers, reciprocity is critical. In order to have a customer trust me, I should be authentic and honest with him or her. I should really want them to benefit; I should trust them. There is no place here for fakes. If I do not respect the customer, if I do not open up to him or her personally; if I do not treat them as a person and not only as a professional, it will be hard to gain their trust. Unless, of course, I find a way to bring them to some extreme situation, as in the ski story at the beginning of this post. This strategy is not recommended!

The journey to trust is long, but the results are very satisfactory. The effort is worthwhile! Not only for the knowledge worker. For me too.

Yours,
    Moria

2008-01-13 07:32

Decision making

There is a well-known Bible story about how the Jewish people left Egypt. Time after time, they ask Pharaoh, the king of Egypt, to set them free, and he insists on holding on to them as slaves. The Lord reached out His hand and punished Pharaoh and Egypt. Ten times we see this cycle: requests to leave, Pharaoh's stubbornness and refusal, and God's punishment. After eight times, Pharaoh's servants understand the situation and advise Pharaoh to change his mind, based on the information they have. Pharaoh insists on making the incorrect decision: "And Pharaoh's servants said unto him: For how long shall this man (Moses) be a snare unto us? Let the men go and serve God their God! Knowest thou not yet that Egypt is lost?" (Exodus, 10,7). The servants already **know**. Pharaoh does not.

Decisions have always been made. We made decisions in the past and we make them today. However, as time passed and as our employees became Knowledge Workers, decision-making became complicated: there are more decisions we cannot make without relying on the information and knowledge of our employees; we also distribute some decision-making to our workers. It is much more difficult to manage and control decisions made by our employees.
These are the issues I wish to discuss in my post.

Three main points, independent, but interconnected, characterize decision-making, whether by me or by my employees:
First, people make many decisions. Job descriptions are widely defined, and employees are expected to decide for themselves on many daily issues.
The second point deals with the information and knowledge supporting the decision making process. We are overwhelmed with data, information

and knowledge. The worker, while making a decision, or even when bringing us information needed for our decision-making, filters the proposed information, focusing only on the most relevant parts as he or she understands them.

Last, but not least, in most cases there are no right or wrong answers. The world is complicated and answers are not black and white. Most alternatives include pros, cons, and many gray variants in between, all influencing the right decision.

As a result, we the managers, have a difficult time trying to control the quality of decisions made by our employees. This is true *a priori*, as in most cases we have less information and knowledge than our employees (and the information we have was filtered en route to us). It is also true *post-priori* , as in many cases we do not have the tools to examine how good the decision was compared to other alternatives. To make a long story short, our life as managers trying to manage the decision making of our employees is not that simple.

I can share several tips from my experience:

a. Do not try to control each decision made. Let the employees act independently; let us focus on controlling only **main** decisions.

b. When trying to control and take part in a decision made, ask not only about the decisions recommended, but also about the **rationale** that prompted this recommendation. A recommended technique for complicated decisions is to request that the employee describe other alternatives, including their pros and the reasons why after all they were not recommended.

c. Observe, along time, the high level decision making mechanisms of the employees, to be sure they know how to make decisions. Maybe even bring someone in to tutor them. We should remember that decision-making is a central part of our employees' job.

Easy? Not at all. Possible? Of course. I can say that it is wrong to try and make decisions for our employees. It is tempting, but forbidden. Making decisions through our employees is right professionally, and is part of their personal development. Sometimes, our employees will make decisions contrary to what we think is correct. In most cases, however, this is not an excuse for changing the decision and overriding them. This is not an easy process (I can speak for myself that it is not at all easy to stop myself from telling them what to do!) but it is part of being a manager of a Knowledge Worker.

Who said life is boring?

Yours,
    Moria

Antoly Yudochsky, 01/23/2008, 17:23

One psychological theory says that one should give a person a feeling that his every decision, even one that turns out to be not so successful, can be improved or changed in the future. This is to reduce the huge pressure he feels when making decisions. After all, just as you wrote here, all of us need to make decisions every day, some of which are considered the most fundamental and crucial. Actually, this is not so. A person who prepared well and arrived at a decision after careful consideration should not have to worry about having made a mistake or bad decision. Again you were correct here, because there is no black and white. Any solution contains within it more and less successful parts. The main thing is to learn from both. And the research attained after receiving the results is more important in most cases than the decision itself. New management methods, like AGILE, help a lot here, as they let you perform systematic research, which is controlled but also includes a lot of FUN as part of the process.

Learning by teaching

In the coming week, I am starting another series of our Knowledge Management course. Theoretically, I could have mixed emotions: happy that another fully booked course is starting; delighted, as a champion of the field, that another group is learning the secrets of the trade; but disappointed, as I have to repeat a task in which I teach the same content so many times, over and over again. This is not really the situation and actually the opposite is true. Dave Snowden shares with us, in his blog, "The Cognitive Edge" in the post "Musings between flights," how surprised he is that he never gets bored when he teaches some material repeatedly. Every time the audience changes his experience, and his ideas are refined. I could not agree more. I have given the opening lecture of the course "Introduction to Knowledge Management" maybe one hundred times already, but it still improves almost every time. Moreover, not only is the lecture getting better, but my understanding of how to deal with people and organizations and how knowledge is to be managed also improves.

We learn when we teach. In a similar manner, we learn when we write an article or a summary on a topic. When writing, or speaking up in front of an audience, we have to organize our thoughts, and by doing so, we build another layer of knowledge. (see Nonaka and Takeuchi's *The Knowledge Creating Company*, where they discuss the internalization stage in developing new knowledge). When we give a lecture and the audience asks questions or comments about it, they make us think; they sharpen our understanding. Teaching is an important learning instrument.

Learning, one may even say continuous learning, is a significant part of our employees' job. The changing reality, the developing technologies and the mass of information force our employees to learn and develop repeatedly, and adapt the way they perform their jobs in light of what they learn. Those who do not advance, retreat.

Life, however, is not that simple. How and when can we enable our employees to teach as part of their learning process?

I will start with the bottom line. There is no one answer. This dilemma requires gentle balance: on the one hand, it is obvious that tutoring or giving lectures will improve our workers. On the other hand, when we stand in front of an audience, we want to give the best we can, and put forward the experts, not the apprentices. Reality is even more complicated: many of my employees know how to lecture, and even do it well. They know the materials thoroughly, and have day-to-day examples, which they have learned from their own experience. Nevertheless, the audience expects what they think is the best: the senior among all seniors.

How should we act? There is no single route.

When giving external lectures and tutoring, I do it myself, or with the help of employees who are already known as experts in the specific field.

I think that inside the organization there is an opportunity to enable learning by teaching: in apprenticeship processes. When enabling employees, and not only the managers and experts, to share their knowledge with new employees, we profit twice:

first, as already stated, by enabling the teacher to learn by teaching, and second, to be aware that in some ways it is easier to learn from non-experts. In their book, *Deep Smarts*, Leonard and Swap explain that it is easier to learn from someone when the gap of knowledge between them and yourself is smaller. We are used to the idea that it is best to learn from the experts. The truth is quite the opposite: when we learn from someone close to us, s/he understands us better, and for us, it is easier to ask questions.

Such a process requires our control, as managers. We have to ensure that the learning process is indeed appropriate, and try not to stand too much in the way, trying to fix it too much.

So who said that our job as managers is boring?

Yours,
Moria

2008-02-08 09:05

 # Between acting emotionally and acting rationally

For many years, we were educated to think and act rationally, to be logical and ordered. I, for example, was educated in a very strict high school and things got even more logical and rational during my university years in the Mathematics and Computing department. No doubt that rational management has significant benefits: it enables consistent progress towards company goals; it enables the existence of uniform processes in organizations; it enables control.

In contrast, there is a saying about sales that states that 80% of every sale is emotional and only 20% rational.
Even if we think this saying is exaggerated and radical, we must acknowledge that a substantial portion of every sale is indeed emotional.

Last week I took part in a convention dealing with decision making. Most presentations were based on games theory, psychology of decision making and the combination of both. The main theme was that in decision-making we combine rational and emotional processes.

I wish to claim that emotional and rational combined management is not a constraint or weakness. Emotional and rational combined management is **better**. I am sure that some may think (and they may be correct) that what I say is exactly the proof that cognitive dissonance works. Maybe I am trying to justify myself, as I act in this way.

Yet here are some points in favor of emotional management and its combination with rational management:
a. We work with people, whether customers, suppliers, managers or employees. In a knowledge era, more people work for a greater

41

portion of their time with other people. The best way to work with people is to be a person: to speak to those we work with, not only as professionals, but rather as people. To be sensitive to others. To support and take interest in what they go through. Not to be arrogant. Combining emotional aspects enables me to express "me."

b. Intuition seems to be the opposite of rational management - decisions based on "gut feeling," not brains. However, when examining the issue more carefully, we understand that the experts, those who have much experience, rely a lot on intuition. They make many decisions without even thinking. Even when they analyze alternatives, many times the first alternative considered turns out to be the best. That is intuition. How does intuition work? Maybe the decisions are not really "gut feeling" decisions. The expert does think, does analyze and does decide rationally. He or she runs this process unconsciously and therefore we have the illusion that it was emotional and not rational.

c. The main point is that combining emotional and rational management aspects provides a broader view. It enables us to take into consideration not only what is profitable, but also what is right to do. Emotional thinking often gives us the opportunity to think not only "business," but also "values." Emotional management does not necessarily mean getting angry and acting impulsively, exposing our weak points. Emotional management is, first and foremost, doing what is right in our eyes (even if it is not done "by the book").

I have been fortunate enough to run my own firm. Managing in my own terms, I do not have any directorate urging me to concentrate only on financial profits. I can act by involving emotions and logic, and no one can complain. Yes, I am lucky. I thank God every day for that.

Yours,
 Moria

Andy, 08/25/2008, 7:00
Your following statements strongly align with my own life experiences;
Emotional thinking gives us the opportunity, many times, to think not only
"business," but also "values."
Emotional management does not necessarily mean getting angry and
acting impulsively, externalizing all our weak points.
Emotional management is first and foremost, doing what is right in our
eyes (not only regarding our conscious brain).

I work in the high pressure environment of operational emergency
services and our greatest challenge so far is combining emotional and
rational management so that we can predict safe systems of work, yet
take account of diverse belief when planning how we arrange our
working practices and training.
I have evolved my own way of managing people which seems to go down
well. I aim to encourage individual emotion and then provide a conduit to
make it work for the team. This requires a lot of people skills so I'm not
sure everyone could do it. What do you think?
Andy

From evaluation to feedback

It is not that easy to manage knowledge workers. As discussed, knowledge workers are very independent. In their specific jobs, they have more expertise than we, as their managers, have. The knowledge workers even decide when to share knowledge with us, and how much will be shared. This is normative. This is their job. Nevertheless, it does not make our job of management and control easy or simple.

Once a year, many organizations evaluate the performance of their workers. This activity is not a substitute for the ongoing evaluation process that takes place all year long, as we comment, thank and appreciate our workers. The yearly evaluation is different. We stop to think, and give an overall evaluation, which is written down. The yearly evaluation has ceremonial importance.

The evaluation process. We are not aware of most of what our workers do on a daily basis. In places where we are, many times we hear what they do through their perspective, as they are the ones to report. In the specific job they are in charge of, they are the experts. This is what makes them knowledge workers. Performance is not measured only quantitatively. The bottom line - the evaluation is not an easy task.

The problem is clear, so what could and should be done?
I shall start by confessing: I have evaluated many workers, knowledge workers. I have tried evaluating based on wide overseeing. I have tried evaluating based on qualitative measures and not only quantitative ones. I have tried using many techniques. Sometimes I succeeded. There are workers that listened, understood, even thanked me and changed. But the truth has to be said: more times, I failed. Workers, in the evaluation session, always had answers to whatever I commented on. They knew how to describe instances where their behavior was opposite to what I explained. Workers found different meanings to shared reality. Workers

did not agree with what was said. Workers did not understand. In some cases, they decided to ignore. I have seen it all. I have been hurt and disappointed; them too.

This all, until a wise person taught me how to turn the evaluation process into a feedback process. I know this is not possible in all organizations (or at least in its full transition), yet, wherever possible, even partly, I think it is worth considering.

First, let us redefine the goal of this process: not evaluating, rather directing the worker; helping him or her to work better. No one is perfect, and each one of us does some things better, some things worse. We all have room for improvement. As part of the process, it is the right time also to appreciate. As stated earlier, this is an activity with ceremonial aspects, and appreciation here has its importance. Nevertheless, this is not the main goal. The main issue is helping the worker improve.

Several insights to think about:

a. We are speaking about a feedback process, not evaluation.
b. Although we may know about many faults and behaviors that need improvement, we focus only on two or three. People are not capable of internalizing too many changes simultaneously.
c. It is not wise to concentrate on the most prominent behaviors. Rather, what affects the worker's performance should be considered.
d. Certain things are hard to change. We are not in a justice process, rather in an improvement one. We have to focus only on weaknesses that can be improved.
e. Every feedback has to be accompanied with a practical way for implementing the change. If I do not have such an idea, sometimes I will not give the comment at all. Yet the decision how to change belongs to the workers themselves. We have to give them one alternative; they will decide whether to implement the change based on this alternative or on any other path they choose.

In addition, one last tip. When preparing the feedback, think of the organization's values. These values are there to direct us in the correct direction. They were constructed in order to lead us to the organization's vision. The values are to be examined, and the weaknesses, like points of appreciation, are to be derived from them.

Do these directions improve the process of evaluation? I believe so, but some years have to go by before it can be shouted loud and clear. Will it always bring success? Of course not, but the chances will be better.

Moving from evaluation to feedback improves the process, improves the output, but also makes it easier for us, as managers of knowledge workers, since we cannot fully evaluate the performance of our workers.

Being a manager is a complicated task. Complicated, but challenging and rewarding.

Yours,
   Moria

Esti Doron, 03/10/2008, 10:14
I really identified with what was written here. I am connected to the educational field and have been experimenting over the past two years in constructive evaluation in the style of CLINICAL SUPERVISION. Each time I am surprised anew by the power of the constructive feedback, by the reflections that teachers are able to make about themselves if they are only asked the questions rather than told what the right thing is to do and how to do it. The same principles that work in a feedback session with a knowledge worker also work with teachers (workers in the educational field). Every tip you recommend is successfully tried out in the field of education.

Ilan Sharif, 05/22/2008, 10:25

I definitely like this approach: not to think what is right, but rather what works, to think of the person on the other side. Can you add a post regarding the way to manage the feedback files, or, in brief, how to preserve what was discussed in the feedback conversation? Especially in organizations in which no appropriate software exists and it must be done with simple "MS Office" tools, is it worth it to draw up an appropriate form? How does one input what was discussed in the previous feedback conversation? Should the manager and worker have common access to the document?

Asking

The Jewish people read the "Haggada" on Passover. The story within speaks about four sons: the wise boy, the evil one, the naive and the boy that does know how to ask. Wise and evil, are easy to understand; maybe we even follow when the "Haggada" speaks about the naive; but why "The boy that does not know how to ask?"

Knowing to ask is a skill that is basic for learning. Without curiosity, without seeking what is missing in an existing product, service, or even situation, it is difficult for us, as workers and as people, to advance from the present towards the future.

I wish to focus in this post on the issue of asking, from the perspective of being a manager.

The technique of asking questions can help us as managers serve various needs:

Asking as a tool for control.

Knowledge workers are independent workers. We, as their managers, are not involved in their daily work and cannot always see the full picture of the activities of which they are in charge. Furthermore, as I have already written in the past, we understand less than they do in some of their areas of work and expertise. Asking questions can assist control in two ways:

a. Asking can assist in emotional matters, as part of understanding how our employees feel as human-beings and not only as workers. The trivial questions, "what's new?," "how do you feel?" or "what's up?" have become ways of saying "hello," or "good morning." Most people do not answer these questions with care, and even when they do, most askers do not listen to what has been said. We, as managers, are responsible for knowing how our employees really feel and to look out for them, especially when it is not a shiny day. Our responsibility as managers is to ask, to mean it when we ask and to listen to the answer.

b. Asking can assist in professional matters, as part of understanding where issues stand and maybe where problems exist. Even if we understand less than our employees, a few innocent questions can point to holes in solutions, where people are not too sure. Overconfidence, like lack of confidence, are obvious clues for places where we should probably probe further. I remember myself, twenty-five years ago, as a math student. The professor was standing near the board, showing us a mathematical proof. One hundred students were sitting silently, trying to catch up with him. Then, he suddenly stopped, thought for a minute or even less, and continued filling up the board. After he finished, I raised my hand and asked him to explain the line where he had stopped five minutes earlier. He looked at the board for a minute and erased all he had written. I did not mean harm, but I felt that something was wrong, by the message passed by his behavior. People tell us in so many ways; we have the task of listening.

Asking as a tool of guiding and teaching.

The technique of asking questions as a tool for guiding other people, or even advancing on ourselves, is familiar and has been used for decades. It is a significant element of the reflection process, where we go out (mentally), and look at things from outside the situation, ask questions regarding it, and understand how to perform better.

There are two main advantages in using the technique of asking questions as a tool for guiding and teaching:

a. If we as managers ask our employees questions and leave the answering part to them, we diminish the resistance that can grow in some cases, when we use other techniques. It is not easy for any of us to absorb criticism, and if the questions are indeed innocent and not dissembling, this technique of asking questions may turn out to be effective.

b. Asking questions open minds. Here we give our employees the tools to become even more professional than they are now. This, after all, is the essence of guiding.

There are many other situations in which we as managers should ask questions: when planning strategy; when planning any future; when selling (whether ideas in the organization or products and services to our out-of-the-organization customers). Actually, asking may assist in almost every process we carry out.

There have been times when employees would come to me and ask, and I would answer. Nowadays, I try to hold myself back (and believe me, it is not that easy for me) and respond with a question: What do you think? What are the alternatives? Why? Of course, this takes more time in the short term, and everyone who knows me personally will testify that I never have time. But I try remind myself that this is the proper way to act, and surely, in the long term, it takes less time, not more. I try holding myself back. Sometimes, I even succeed.

Before ending this post, I want to leave you with some open questions for further thought:
How much to ask? Asking too much is a burden.
How to ask? Asking in the wrong way is worse than not asking at all. Do not patronize; do not dissemble; do not ask "closed" questions; do not ask too "open" questions (if the target is guiding, some guiding has to take place in the question).
Moreover; it is important to understand when it is wrong to ask questions. Sometimes we must just leave our employees with space. They need it (as we do).
Your opinion would be appreciated.

Yours,
Moria

Avi Zucker, 03/25/2008, 12:49

Great post in time for Passover. You might also mention the youngest of the participants who asks questions during the Passover "seder" and receives four different answers to one question, answers from which we can learn what we need to know about why this night is different from all other nights. Even if some of the respondents are lacking some information, they attain that information by working through the questions together. Cooperation (forced, structured, ceremonial – but effective) between the asker and the respondents contributes to the general knowledge and shortens processes.

Democracy

The origin of the word democracy comes from Greek (Δημοκρατία), and its literal translation to English is "rule of the people." Indeed, this translation guides us as to what democracy really means.

A business organization is no democracy. It is ruled by the shareholders and their representatives, and is managed by a small group elected for that purpose. The managers are those that make decisions - not "the people."

Winston Churchill once said that "democracy is the worst way for ruling, expect for all other ways that were already experienced." Like other things said by him, this is a wise sentence. Even though democracy is not a good way to rule (a country), other ways are worse.

Usage of the term democracy has expanded, and does not serve us only in the political region. We use it in many other cases as a way of speaking about making decisions based on the majority.

Many times we ask ourselves why we don't succeed in building the same atmosphere of will and passion in the organization as people have for home, friends, sports and other areas outside the office. The issue has many perspectives. Let us look, for example, at blogging. We see people blogging and collaborating outside work, much more than in work. I am cautious. This is not an issue of black and white. People do not suffer at work. I hope that in most organizations people do not dislike the place in which they work. Yet there are differences between the office and outside it, and there is certainly place for improvement. The more our office is a place to which our employees want to come every morning, the more they stay (and that in itself is worth a lot). But more importantly, if people like the place where they work - they perform better.

Enabling people to make decisions indeed helps. We like to be involved; we like to have influence on others. This is reciprocal: the more the organization enables employees to be involved and to influence, the more the employees give of themselves.

Let us remember, though, that we are a business, a place with defined business goals. Making decisions based on a majority can contradict with shareholders' favor. The process of making decisions, involving many people, takes much more time than if only a small group is involved.

Many organizations therefore find other ways for satisfying their employees, and leave democracy out of the organization's door.

However, it is important to understand that the benefits of sharing in the process of decision-making go far beyond the involvement and good feelings of the employees.

Professionally, it is better to make decisions by asking many people. This is the wisdom of the crowds. This term, coined by James Surowiecki back in 2004, is also the title of a book written by him. From the book's full name ***The Wisdom of Crowds: Why the Many Are Smarter Than the Few and How Collective Wisdom Shapes Business, Economies, Societies and Nation*** we can understand the relevance to our topic - democracy in decision-making. Consulting more people brings better results. We have learned this from Wikipedia, which has become the leading Encyclopedia worldwide, and from many experiments performed comparing the wisdom of experts and the wisdom of crowds. Every time we are surprised again to see that in most cases crowd beats experts.

The bottom line: it is beneficial for organizations to involve employees in decision-making.

When and how?

In decisions that are related to new ideas for strategic moves;

In decisions related to forecasting market trends and desires;

In organizational decisions related to the people as a group (where there is no conflict of interest between the people, or between them and the organization);

When designing user interfaces of products;

Where brainstorming is needed in order to understand a problem or suggest solutions.

The criteria: where information is not classified; where quality is essential; where it is worthwhile comparing to resources (time, cost); where our future lies.

I, as the owner and manager of a company, became, in the first years of the company, accustomed to deciding on my own. As time passed, I learned to involve larger groups of people. The sharing may take many formats: sometimes as the first stage, sometimes in consulting on the way, sometimes in openness to changes - after the initial decision has been made. In some cases, the group is larger; in others, two or three people take part. There is no one recipe for success.

The name of the game, as in so many other areas, is to work gradually; important when attempting to succeed manage the change in an existing organization.

The personal indecision is always there: fast versus comprehensive; wisdom of experts versus wisdom of the crowds. We, as managers, have to decide - when alone, when with a small group and when as a democracy.

At the end of the day, we will be those to pay or profit. We will have to be responsible. Responsibility is no democracy. It remains ours.

Yours,
  Moria

 Alon Sherer, 04/01/2008, 12:58

Shalom Moria,

I think you have touched on a very important point, which has several advantages - the involvement and commitment of employees, seizing leadership and strategy. The habit of listening and accepting things that are not ours is the most effective way to create outside the box thinking. We should of course listen to all kinds of people, not just those that we enjoy listening to. Here, the rule that says I need to find a way I can agree with any claim before I decide in its favor is very helpful.

For the employees, on the other hand, self-expression is very important (especially for professionals); they want to see practical implementation - those places where their opinion has become fact in the company. It is important that the actions or the progress towards the shared vision be shared by the employees.

All this makes life more complex, but certainly creates satisfaction and a considerable improvement in the parameters of quality and commitment.

 # People

I have a long drive today, as I am giving a lecture somewhere far away. A long trip means a lot of time for thoughts. My thoughts are wondering, thinking about a friend, a customer, who just underwent a significant surgery. Will she recover? When? The questions stand open, and no one has an answer. The hours go by, and we are all waiting. Tense.
People.
Yesterday, several people told me that they are looking for a job, as their organization is reducing its workforce. Last week I spoke with another colleague, who spoke about a near re-organization, and again, a reduction in force. For two or three months now, everything seems sad there. Even though in his division there is a lot of work to be accomplished, people are not as they were in the past. They leave early, speak quietly, and every week a few more people leave, having found themselves a new place to work. My heart is with the people laid off; my heart is with the people who have to fire others.
People.

In the 21st century, it seems as if we have become more sophisticated; advertisements and ratings have led us to places we did not dream of. Communication and media consultants of politicians produce strategy and we stare and do not believe. Is everything fake? Where does reality stop?

In this same century, working relations have changed radically. In this information and knowledge era, we are to give more of ourselves: not only our time (which seems to be 24 hours of work with cellular phones and laptops); not only our brain (even a more precious resource); but also our hearts. People who work technically only, succeed less. Work in the 21st century is comprised of partnership: partnership while working in teams in the organization; partnership while working with suppliers; and partnership, real win-win situations, working with customers. Every other alternative will leave us far behind.

This behavior triggers an opening. The way from opening to exposure is short. We enable other people, who we normally would lock out of our thoughts after 17:00, to stay in our hearts 24 hours a day. When they hurt, we hurt; of course, it is much easier, to be happy when they are too.

We become less strong and more vulnerable. But we also become better human-beings. People. Purified.

Steve Jobs spoke this week at the graduation ceremony of Stanford University. Listen to what he said:

(http://www.youtube.com/watch?v=D1R-jKKp3NA). He shared three personal stories in which he exposes himself being adopted, dropping out of university, walking once a week seven miles to have a decent meal, his cancer, his being fired from Apple. All these stories are relevant. Their purpose is not to make people feel sorry for him or to think he is a hero. They all are part of guides to life that he tries to share with the graduating students.

I think we are blessed to live in such an era. The risk of being vulnerable comes together with great chance. I am not speaking of the chance of greater success. That too though. The bigger chance is personal for each and every one of us as a person. As a human-being.

We are lucky. Work may on take over our personal lives; but work in these conditions helps us be people.

Educate your workers to be people; Let us all be people with whomever we work and not only with our friends back home.

Let us wish everyone health.

Yours,
    Moria

P.S. Day after: to all those who wish to know, my friend is better; the surgery succeeded.

P.S. Eighteen months later (publishing the book): Sorry to share, but this friend passed away.

 Ami Salant, 04/10/2008, 13:53
Thanks for the value-laden perspective. It is important
Ami Salant

Simon, 04/10/2008, 14:39
Moria,
I really liked this.
Each of us can find reflections of these things inside (reflections that create internal resonance which, by its nature, increases…)
By the way - this is precisely the secret of books / good writers (one my true loves of life is reading books).
There is immense power in the personal note - mainly because it works on our "computer analogy" – our emotional "thinking."
Personally, I really believe that managing people with a strong emphasis on the emotional component is - from experience - the most powerful.

2008-04-24 21:58

 # Innovation

"Innovation distinguishes between a leader and a follower" (Steve Jobs).
No doubt, we all want to be innovators; we want to be leaders. We want the organization we work in to be innovative. Innovation is, by all standards, a key for business success. Moreover, it is exciting to work in an organization that innovates; much more so than to work in a conservative organization that never changes.

Innovation, however, is not as trivial as we would expect. Continuous innovation may even contradict the concept of knowledge re-use. One of the challenges that few people have dealt with is how to define when it is right to re-use, and when innovation is preferred.

Innovation is not as trivial as we would expect. Because innovation involves not only hiring a good consultant and setting up an innovation team, resulting by the year's end in a new product or service. Innovation is a way of life. Innovation is something ongoing, part of the routine, not a project with a beginning, some time and an end. Innovation is something we would want employees to have in their blood; not only one exceptional, excellent employee, or one group of managers - rather all of them.

Innovation is not trivial, as it is not only related to products, but rather is relevant to various organizational layers: operational innovation; innovation in processes; innovation in products or services; strategic innovation; and innovation in management.

Innovation is not trivial, as it really can not be managed. It relates to culture. Therefore many steps can be taken in the right direction- but the overarching aim is nurturing the continuous innovation and not creating it.

The task of explaining innovation, its components and how to facilitate it, is complicated and suitable for a book rather than a post. However, I think it is possible to share some of the tools I use in the organization I manage in order to nurture and encourage innovation.

There are two types of activities: practical and cognitive. Both are important and I do not believe one can be skipped.

Practical activities include:

a. Working in teams; small teams that enable discussion and strengthen innovation.

b. Employing different people to work together on the same team/project/type of job. Formal job role definition may lead us to the "ultimate" Assignments of people to work I learned that there is no such thing. Several years ago, I found myself employing female managers, one after the other, with two many similar characteristics to my own: mission oriented and very energetic. Today, the staff is heterogeneous: heterogeneous in their characteristics, heterogeneous in their education (for the same job) and heterogeneous in their life experience.

c. I make an effort to assign each employee to more than one project (in parallel), and as much as possible, to different types of projects, with different contexts. I make an effort to mix people, so that every employee has the chance to work with and see different perspectives of different employees.

d. I make an effort to enable my employees to be independent, by distributing the power and the decisions. I encourage the managers under me to act in the same way.

e. We professionally enrich all workers on a regular basis (twice a month - six hours altogether). The things we teach and share include practical knowledge together with higher-level knowledge, knowing that what is not relevant for the employee today, will help him or her tomorrow - on a different project, or in understanding and seeing more perspectives than today.

f. We demand of our employees to share new knowledge and good ideas on a monthly basis. When the company was small, we did it as part of our face-to-face meetings. As the company grew, this became very impractical, and we renewed the sharing in other routine formats.

However, beside the practical activities, there is the cognitive perspective.

The cognitive perspective includes:

a. Us recognizing, as managers, that knowledge and ability do exist, and mainly in the field. The first consequence of such understanding is that everyone has to spend some part of his or her time in the field, including all managers, top down. The second consequence is recognizing (and this is not as simple as it sounds) that our employees, even though they are younger, even though they have less experience, still are those to innovate. Not tomorrow, rather today. Moreover, they not only add new knowledge but also contradict what we did successfully yesterday. It indeed took me, dealing with Knowledge Management for so many years, some time to open myself to learning from my employees. The change was in me.

b. The employees recognizing that innovation is expected and even demanded of them. Innovation is not only a nice value declared as part of the company's mission and strategy, rather it has practical implications. Recognizing that innovation is a right, that innovation is an obligation, enables and eases the minds to start innovating.

More than anything, personal example is required. Never, never stop renewing and innovating oneself. Innovation is an organizational engine for growth, but not less a personal growth engine.
It contributes to me, and a lot.

Yours,
Moria

Simon, 05/25/2008, 17:13

I have found that I try to implement a few of these suggestions intuitively (or maybe just on the basis of life experience... I believe "intuition" improves with the accumulation of life experience).

I want to share an amazing tool that I am excited to have started to use. You already know the FREEMIND, which I used extensively until now.

I decided to look for a more organized tool in this area of MIND MAPPING.

I found the MindManager. I played with the trial version and then I purchased it.

Its capabilities and options are amazing. One of its most prominent advantages is its solid integration with the Office package - amazing really.

2008-05-14 17:13

 # Time management

Most of us are in a rush. We are always busy. We have to prepare a proposal for the day before yesterday, to give an answer to an open question for our boss, and we are three hours late, and still have to accomplish another mission within one day. We live in a "no time" reality. Once, we used to believe that this is a result of the bubble age, but the bubble exploded and still we have no time. Still, we experience requests "ASAP"; yet in every project, we work around the clock up until the due date and many times, even after.

Lee Iacocca, the former CEO of the Chrysler Corporation, once said that the ability to concentrate and smartly take advantage of time is everything.

Without being as smart or as successful as Iacocca, I could not agree more. I feel, on a personal level, that time is a most precious resource, and in some cases, more important even than money.

Time is a misleading resource. On one hand, it is limited: there are only 24 hours in every day. On the other hand, many times, those people who seem to be busier than others find the time to take on additional responsibilities, much more than other, less busy people.

As managers, it is important to manage time, twofold:

Firstly, the knowledge work is characterized by handling many tasks and working in parallel. Even if we are under the impression that we are handling one task, this task usually includes many sub-tasks, and these do not tend to be processed one after the other. We, as managers, surely have more than a handful of tasks.

Secondly, we manage people who have to know how to manage their time by themselves. It has already been written that knowledge workers manage their own routine. We, as their managers, have to give them the right tools to manage their time, and to find ways to assure they actually do so.

63

A few tips I can share for managing time, based on my own experience:

- Understanding that feeling busy and being busy are not exactly the same thing. One of the reasons that some people tend to overload themselves with additional tasks, and succeed in carrying them out, is based on them not perceiving themselves as having no time. Coping with the feeling of "no time," is sometimes more demanding that actually having no time.

- Defining regular and steady hours in which we read and handle Emails. Reading every Email as it arrives disturbs and interferes with our concentration. It harms both the source task being produced and the Email itself.

- Defining in advance (and teaching employees to do the same) the time we are willing to invest in performing every task that is meant to take longer than an hour. We often tend to invest more in order to achieve the highest quality possible. In many cases it is not worth the effort. In other words, we put more than the organization, or the customer, wants us to. As in other situations, dear Pareto plays a significant role (father of 20:80 rule) in advising us where to stop. It is not good enough, though, only to plan efforts. We must ensure that we do as plan. We must not only plan, but also finish tasks within the timeframe defined. Defining time is already a first step in helping us better manage our time. Our will to fulfill is the second step. Performance is the third.

- Working on tasks and completing them as soon as they arrive (after finishing the previous ones already started). I usually say that starting earlier does not mean I spend more time on a task. The opposite is true. When the issue is fresh, it is easier and faster for us to work on it and complete it. We also save the time of managing all open tasks if we keep a clean table.

- Ensuring that we leave time for handling not only the urgent, but the important as well. Handling the urgent wears us out. Handling important tasks is sometimes more imperative, both for the organization and for us as individuals.

- Defining timeframes in the calendar for working on tasks that we do not find any other time for completing. If, every time we think things get out of control, we are strict with ourselves and do not repeatedly cancel these self meetings, we can occasionally clear our table, and restart better managing our time.

In addition, one last tip: See that your people take vacations. For us, as an organization, it is cheaper that they work and we pay them for these vacation days. For their sake, ensure that they really take vacations. These will give them the strength to go on. That also is part of time management.

Some wise person (unknown) once said: "Two facts about time management: a) you cannot control the time you are born or the time in which you die. b) all points between the two are negotiable."

Probably we can control most. Let us take advantage of this and do so.

Yours,
    Moria

 Paul, 05/16/2008, 7:45

Moria,
Great point about "feeling" vs. "being" busy.
The truth is that the stress from "feeling" typically eliminates the possibility of "being" productively busy.

Simon, 05/25/2008, 17:13
Moria,
I really liked this blog – smart insights, which are nice, but even more important, practical too.

Encouraging the doing

Miguel de Cervantes Saavedra, a Spanish novelist, poet, and playwright, is well known to many of us as the author of the one of the kind book: *Don Quixote*. This is not the only book written by him, but indeed the most influential one. In his book, Saavedra writes: "There is a big difference between speaking and doing."

If we are honest with ourselves, we will find that all of us, as managers, workers and private people, are living examples. We all know that there are things that should be done and even though we are aware we do not behave accordingly. We know about techniques and methodologies that proved successful, and yet we do not take action.

What makes us concentrate on speaking rather than on doing? What makes us know more and implement less? How can we be sure that our employees do more than speak? In an era of knowledge, when we rely on what our employees decide to share, and we can only partly control what actually is done and achieved, it is important to give them and ourselves the tools to encourage doing, and better balance speaking and doing.

I think I always tried to practice what I preach. Enough? Probably not. A book that I read over a year ago, *The Knowing Doing Gap*, written by Jeffrey Pfeffer and Robert Sutton, is my guide to this never-ending dilemma.

Why do people tend to speak rather act? There are several reasons:

Firstly, we appreciate people who speak. Sometimes even more than those who do: speaking wisely is here and now; results of doing are observed only later;

Because speaking outlines the message; it takes some thinking to understand the messages behind the acting;

Because people who speak (if they do not exaggerate) are thought of as people who influence and in some cases, even as leaders;

Because in colleges and universities in management programs we talk and write, but hardly actually do;
And, because most of us were appointed to our jobs after mainly our speaking skills were checked.

Secondly, we were all brought up learning that planning is essential before acting, and that the more we plan, the less we need to work on doing. In some projects, we use up all resources of time, money and management care, and yet we remain in the planning phase.

Furthermore, it is easier to speak than to do; it requires less energy.

The list is of reasons why to speak rather act is not short. I will just add that it is very challenging to change existing habits of work in order to do new things. Leading the change is so difficult that in some cases we convince ourselves that if we speak, we also implement. Are organizational activities of building a vision and sets of values, actually turning the vision and values into reality? Is a manager stating in the company board meeting that innovation is important actually implementing innovation? And there are many more examples.

A few tips that assist in assuring that we will also act and not only speak:
- Pay attention to the balance between meetings and doing; pay attention to the balance between documents (presentations, white papers) and fieldwork.
- Implement the organization's values and turn them into reality; they are probably guiding us in the right direction.
- Promote mainly workers from inside the organization; bring less managers from the outside. Encourage the incentives of employees to act.
- Assure that every manager works on the field level and does not purely manage others, just remembering the fieldwork from the past.
- Speak simply. It is okay to have a complicated idea if it can be explained in simple words and can be translated into simple actions.

If people understand what is expected from them, there is a good chance they will actually do it.

- Distribute responsibility and authority; be patient of resulting mistakes. People will not act if they are to be punished when they err.
- Prevent measuring results of the individual employee. If we must measure, measure processes of work rather than results. Measure teams rather than individuals. By doing so we encourage work within teams (that is so important in the era of knowledge workers). Measuring only results may trigger short-term benefits, but can damage and act as a boomerang in the long term. How to measure the individual? Measure them in how they comply with the organization's values.
- Prevent competition inside the organization. Most competitions are zero sum games and if someone wins, we have others that lose. We all know that competition is a trigger for motivating people and we all have examples that prove it (i.e. in sports). Competition is important? Encourage outside competition.
- Nurture learning through workshops and hands-on experiencing. Lectures deal with speaking. Teach people through doing. He who learns from doing – does.

In addition, a last tip. I personally prepared a short list based on these guidelines and it appears before me every day, pasted on the wall in my study room. At least, once a month, I check myself to see that I did not become an over-speaker in one way or another.

What benefits will we reap? First, more doing. Later on, more self-satisfaction. And in the end, probably better performance, for our organization, our families (if we took the tips in that direction) or, if we are lucky, then both. It is worthwhile. Try it.

Yours,
    Moria

2008-06-11 21:05

 # Company values

Twenty years ago, I had a first opportunity to manage a group of (knowledge) workers. I served in the army in a computing unit of the Israeli Air Force. One day, a new commander arrived. He had new ideas that seemed very odd to us back then. A few weeks after he arrived the building was filled with big signs reading: "Quality counts." Today, twenty years later, I understand the rationale behind this move. At the time, I did not and I was not the only one. No one explained. The signs turned into a joke, and so did the commander.

Years passed by, and methods became more sophisticated. We started to see visions and missions in organizations we worked in, and we took part in teams that helped define parts of them. I cannot say that a vision existed in every organization I worked in. Some organizations dealt with these issues while others did not. I cannot even state that there was any correlation between immediate business success and the existence of company vision and values.

A few years ago, I decided that the company that I established could be considered an organization (we reached 10 employees). We were mature enough to have our own vision and company values. We worked thoroughly on definitions. I handed in the first draft, rather excitedly, to one of the company founders, who was not involved in the daily activities. His response was rather chilly: Why deal with values? Rather deal with numbers. And do not misunderstand: the company was profitable.

This is a real dilemma. Is there place for vision and company values in 21st century organizations? Is their importance or position now different to what they were?

I spent many hours dealing with this issue. This founder was a special man, a leader that managed several organizations and has strategic thinking. Yet something important had been said. It could not be ignored. I examine the society in which we live - a society that seems to be materialistic and hedonist, a society in which cynicism is praised. Is there place in such a society for company values?

The truth must be said. As much as I thought about the issue, I had and have no doubt that company values are a necessity. Values are the road signs, guiding us to appropriate work and behavior, both as managers and as workers. Moreover, today in the 21st century, I feel that we need them more and not less. People move from one job to another. They have no one career and of course no one working place. People, wiser than me, have discovered that what keeps an employee in the organization is not salary. Of course, salary has to be fair. Otherwise, the dissatisfaction will be so great that nothing else will be considered. People, despite the materialistic shell, want to work in a place where they feel good. Feeling good is a consequence of the nearby environment - the team, and the larger environment - the organization. Feeling good means they work in a place with which they identify, and of which they are proud to be a part. This is where the company values come in. The forbidden and "musts" are defined by regulations and procedure. The right and justified, the appropriate, are defined by the company values. If we do not have values, we are just a bunch of workers sitting in the same place; little will connect us to each other. Such organizations will experience difficulties in retaining employees in the long run.

The process of designing the company values starts in peoples' hearts in the first years of the organization's life, is refined, and becomes instituted within the next years, as the organization grows and builds its unique culture. In fact, writing down the company values is not supposed to invent anything new, rather to document the existing, helping us to focus, assisting us to distinguish between what is important, and what is more important, stating to all employees that this is our way of life.

Here are a few tips I believe in, all having to do with designing and documenting the company values. Some I have learnt the hard way:

- Do not define too many values. Three years ago, we worked on a set of values for our organization. We defined nine values, all reflecting the company's spirit and way of work. One day, recently, I tried to memorize the list. I found out, that I, as the manager of the company, could not remember the whole list. If anyone would test me, I could for sure distinguish between principles that are part of our values and those that are not. Yet I could not remember the whole list! I understood that something is wrong. If I had nine children, I would surely remember all their names. I have twenty employees and I remember all their names. There was no excuse. If the entire list was that important, I should remember it. Today we are in a process of rewriting the values. The process is more difficult than the initial one, as this time we are focused on choosing the most appropriate values from this list. We limited ourselves to four values.
- Share; make people part of the process. Otherwise, they may think that it is all declarations and not something we mean to act upon. This is what I thought twenty years ago when I saw the sign (and I must state that back then I was even part of the management team). If we want people to feel comfortable with the values and we want the values to connect them to the organization, it is obvious that they have to be part of the process. Even though it takes time; even though it comes at the expense of other working activities.
- Make sure that the values are planted in people's hearts. Visibility is important; assuring that the values do not stay on the wall (or in the website) but rather affect practical behaviors is even more important. As part of defining the values, define desired behaviors.
- Last, but not least. I have spent many hours lately going through other companies' lists of values. We all want to be the same. It is natural that all companies want to be professional, but having the same lists brings us back to square one. How do we convince our employees that we have a special organization through the value list? Why should they stay and not move on? Yet the shared values are so correct. Shall we give them up just because other organizations chose them before we did? Examining happy families,

we see that the common is greater than the differences. I recommend adding some values that others have if they really define us as a company, but also leaving place for some unique values that no one else has. All this (and this is the hard part), without adding more values than defined in our limits.

At the end of the day, the values are our company's spirit. Do not be without them.

Yours,
    Moria

2008-06-23 12:36

Specialization

Specialization is considered becoming a professional. Sub-specialization makes us nod our heads and stare with admiration. How far is it right to focus and specialize? Where should we place the limits?

As in former posts, what appears here applies to knowledge workers and may not fit other organizations, which have different characteristics.

In the past, there were mega-organizations that did everything by themselves because they could: they calculated costs and decided that it is cheaper to in-house manage all facilities rather than buying facilities from providers. A fascinating example can be examined in the army: they have their own medical services (and not only for those soldiers offshore in the battle); they have their own garages, responsible for treating the cars that the officers hold. As the years pass, we see a change in attitude as the army and other mega-organizations understand that maybe it is wiser to work with out-sourcing. Partly, this change is triggered by re-calculation of costs. Not less results from management considerations: handling all issues saps our attention and leaves less time for the core issues. I will add that we cannot be the best at everything. Organizational focus has several advantages:

It enables one to be the best in its core focus (boutique rather than supermarket);

It enables one to attain the co-operation from those who specialize in complementary matters - any other way might lead to competition also on the unique and specialized subjects;

It enables the organization to pit the best resources in the right places.

Are there any disadvantages? Of course there are. Every organization serves customers. The customer does not want to order his tea bag from one supplier, the sugar from another and the spoon and mug from the third and fourth suppliers. He wants a cup of tea. When we, as an organization, define our limits of focus, we have to think about ourselves, but nevertheless, also think and define things from our customers' point of view. Where we do not give a complete solution has to be well defined, as must relationships with other suppliers. I will not claim that working with other suppliers is always harmonious, but it sure is possible and, in most cases, beneficial.

The same questions reside inside the organization, and even inside the unit. But here, I believe, the answers are different. Of course we will distinguish the engineering unit from the manufacturing unit; of course the salesman does not deal with bookkeeping. We have reached such levels of specialization, even within the unit, that every mission relies on bringing together many people for every decision. Knowledge working, naturally, will include a high level of collaboration between the members of a group. The question is how much. Too broad, may result in a situation where integration turns into a bottleneck and becomes almost impossible. Involving too many people in each task results in higher costs for each project.

How do we find the right path? We have to enlarge the understanding of knowledge workers, who specialized in defined topics, also to complementary topics. By enlarging the understanding, I mean operatively: to know, to implement and to further develop. Of course, consultancy of experts is recommended, but, on some level, we have to consult them in order to learn from them and know better for ourselves. So next time, we will be able to answer part of the questions by ourselves and just validate our answers with the expert. We speak a lot about the synergy from working in collaboration: understanding complementary expertise enables us to experience synergy with ourselves. And, when turning to consult others, we come with a better starting point. I am not trying to say that sales and engineering should be performed by the same person. We have to decide where we cooperate with others. Yet we should not overspecialize. If every expert will understand a bit more of what the others do, s/he can see a broader picture. The expert will be able to develop more innovative ideas, and will also benefit on the personal level, enriched by the new knowledge and offering better solutions to customers.

Even though the initial drive for understanding others' jobs may be cutting down expenses and management efforts, the main benefit is conceptual, and turns us into better workers.

I can say for myself that I work in knowledge management, a profession that involves organizations' cultural understanding, computing understanding, processes understanding and content understanding. Indeed four different disciplines. I grew up in IT units. I learned math and computer sciences. As the years passed by, I learned to understand and implement the other disciplines too. I always hire people with complementing education and experience, to learn from them and to teach them. I turned myself into a knowledge management expert. Today, I know how to manage changes; I know how to effectively organize content; I understand organizational processes and how to draw in the knowledge close to the existing processes. I think that by combining these different disciplines I can provide a better solution for my customers; nevertheless, the major benefit is mine. The combination enables me to better and more deeply understand each discipline; the combination enlarges my horizons. As a person, I am so far from where I was ten years ago, when I specialized in computers only, although computing expertise is considered prestigious.

I benefited. I believe we all do.

Yours,
    Moria

Social involvement

I have a friend whom I like very much. He likes tigers. Not instead of people, but in addition. A few months ago, I paid him a visit. I brought him a small gift - a tiger mug filled with candies. This person has a collection of tigers (not real ones), and every time I had an opportunity to add a new tiger to the collection, I would explain him why the new one is unique and different from all others. This tiger, I explained, was prepared by developmentally challenged children. The mug is a donation, and we have bought a few dozens mugs from an organization that sees to it that the money will be targeted to the children's wellbeing. My friend was enthusiastic. He started taking pictures of me with the mug. He filmed me as if he was preparing an album, from every possible angle. These things, he said, should become public. Everyone has to know, so others will learn too.

Donations; contribution to others. Are these obligations of the individual only or also an obligation of modern organizations? Should they be carried out secretly or publicized? This post deals with these and other questions.

I live in Israel. Here we have many organizations, public and private, which deal with contribution as part of the formal framework. I admit that I have spent many hours thinking whether this is a right strategy. Contribution has to come from the hearts of people, and not considered as another project that the team has to complete. Nonetheless, I think that contribution is probably a good thing:
Because it is a solution for needs that are so wide that they cannot be carried out only by individuals;
Because it can work in ways that individuals cannot always;
And, because, most importantly, contribution initiated by organizations gives workers, who do not contribute as individuals, the opportunity to do

so. And when they have the opportunity, if they indeed fulfill it with their hearts and emotions, it really does not matter who initiated the move.

How can an organization cause people to contribute from their hearts?
First, many do so without the organization even requesting. They volunteer anyhow, or wanted to do so, and the organization gave them a good opportunity.
Some have no preconceptions about giving to others. Two management tools can help here to open people's hearts: The first is giving the employees the means to influence the process and take an active part in it: let them choose to whom to donate or how to contribute, etc. The second is direct contact with those in need. The satisfaction we get from the another person smiling and thanking us is huge. Not much can be compared to such satisfaction.
There is another group of employees: those not in favor of such activities. Some speak loudly, most do not. Surely, I can say, probably these people exist in most organizations. But these people should have no place and should not be employees in any proper organization! Even if they are professional, even if they know their job, it is better for managers not to choose such people when they hire additional staff. You may ask: why? Every organization is meant to fulfill its mission. In private organizations, this means making profit; in public ones, the mission changes. But in all organizations, excluding charitable organizations, there is a well defined target that is not contribution to society. As an owner of a private organization it is very clear to me that, in order to win, I need the most professional employees I can afford. Nonetheless, I insist, for egoistical reasons, that organizations shall not employ workers who resist contribution to those in need. And more than ever, now in the 21st century, this is right.
We employ knowledge workers, workers whom we have to trust, workers who are in some way self managers. I had a very bad experience, trusting, a few years ago, when an employee betrayed me, leaving with company assets and using them in order to directly compete with the company. We were facing a situation where we were going to lose money, possibly big

money. The end of that story was a good one, as I won in court and damage was halted. You may ask about the relevance of this story to the post, but the connection is simple. The main issue that bothered me was how much I can trust employees in the future, yet ensuring that such a situation will not recur. Once, one can err, but twice?

After much thought I arrived at a clear conclusion: I must continue to trust my employees. I shall not change the way I control their work and suspect future betrayal. I have to find a different way. The way I chose is to employ only workers who have personal experience in contribution to society. Such contribution softens our hearts, and whoever felt the need to help other people and did so without requesting anything in return, can be trusted as a human being. Of course this is not instead of seeking professional people; it is an additional condition. I admit that people, when interviewed, are very confused and do not understand why these kinds of questions are asked. One can see it on their faces. I do not explain. But I know that according to their answers we will know if the person is a potential worker in our company. Until now, this method has proved to work. I believe it will continue.

As I said, egoistical reasons.

Some may notice I used the term "social involvement" and did not speak about "social responsibility," a term commonly used nowadays. I, personally, do not feel comfortable with being responsible. It seems patronizing to me: we, responsible for them. I think that being involved is speaking and doing on the same level as the other. And so it is. We never know what will happen tomorrow and where we will be. Being humble serves well.

Speaking about humility, there is one more issue regarding organizational contribution. Contribution in organizations is hard to implement as a secret. Not speaking too much has a great advantage, not because there is any shame here. Speaking in organizations may help the doing. Yet organizations have to be very careful. Over speaking and over publicizing can result in a situation where we enjoy the publicity, and do not do for the sake of doing.

The end of the story I opened with is that my friend, after all, did not publish the pictures. I was glad. I was left with the "book." The mug and I. For me, that was enough.

Blessing us all, just good.

Yours,
    Moria

Anonymous, 05/08/2009,13:36

Hello Moria:

Thank you for your post on Blogger regarding social involvement. I especially liked your ideas about employees who are contribution-minded. I agree, there is something very satisfying about giving. You like the words, "Social Involvement" versus "Social Responsibility".

After all, volunteering ourselves and services is a personal choice. I like both terms. They are different. To me, also, social involvement is something that should be done on equal footing. However, social responsibility (to me) is the ability gained when we respond to the needs of others. It is this ability to respond to the needs of the human race that makes this world worthwhile.

Moria, I like your thoughts. Email me back sometimes. I live in the USA.

🗨 Changes

Changes: the world around us is changing. It always did, but it seems that in the 21st century, the frequency of these changes is becoming higher and higher. This is true of the world in general, and specifically true in organizations.

Organizations change for several reasons. First of all, the business environment outside the organization is changing. The life cycle of products is shrinking. It is true that products can be designed and manufactured so that they last much longer, but people want to renew. They want to renew because they get tired of the existing product; they want to renew because they want new functionality or different solutions that they are exposed to in advertisements, in the media, or by their friends, other consumers. But that is not all. Technologies change; computing changes; and- our employees change. Not their characteristics, rather their names and faces. If twenty years ago, a person hired to work in an organization at age twenty most probably would stay there until retirement, today we find many people who have more than one career, and most people choose to work in more than one organization during their career.

The bottom line: organizations need to be prepared for many changes, external and internal; organizations need to know how to adjust; organizations need to know how to manage the changes.

One might think that I am speaking about a business - practical change of equipment purchasing, change of processes, change of pricing, etc. No. This is something much deeper: it involves management; it is a change concerning people.

As explained earlier, organizations have always had to change and to know how to change. Nevertheless, nowadays the frequency of changes is higher. Much higher. And there is another issue: nowadays, it is much more complicated to lead a change in organizations. Hiatt and Creasy, in their book *Change Management*, and Surowiecki, in his book *The Wisdom of the Crowds*, speak about this problematic situation, each from a different perspective. In hierarchical organizations, as we were accustomed in the past, employees followed instructions. Today, many employees are knowledge workers. They are responsible for decision making in their area of expertise. The classic hierarchical structure is not the organizational structure in some organizations (i.e. start-ups) and not the power structure in others. No matter how we look at it, people do not just do things because they were instructed to do so. I will add and say that this attitude is even stronger, as many times we have the feeling that the employee decides whether to continue to work in an organization, and not the other way round. It is much easier for the knowledge worker to explain why the change is not relevant for him or her, why it is inapplicable or why the timing is not appropriate.

So, what can one recommend?
Here are a few ideas. Beyond my personal experience and mistakes I have made along the way, I want to acknowledge that I learned a lot from Hiaitt and Creasy's book, which deals with change management.
First, we must understand, as managers, that the personal aspect of changes cannot be managed as one unified process for all employees. Yet it is obvious that it is not practical to run an individual management plan for each and every worker. I recommend analyzing the change management needs, and building a unified plan, or a plan for large segments in the organization (i.e. managers, front line workers). In parallel, give individual treatment to thought leaders, for good or bad. The effort seems to be beneficial: their influence helps move the organization towards the change. And, give individual treatment to feedbacks and to those who give them.

Another recommendation connected to preparing the change: do not impose changes on people. Give them a clue, a hint that a change is near. In some cases, it is a hint regarding the imminent change, with no details;

in others, the hint will be accompanied by knowledge about the content of the change. This tip is not as easy to implement as it may seem. The organization starts speaking about the change. Since we did not announce it yet (we are preparing), more is hidden and unknown. People will tend to guess, and damage can occur. Therefore, the time of the preparation hints should be adjacent to the time of the beginning of the change. The professional term is "unfreeze." This tip is also relevant for personal changes. Preparation eases the move.

As we are speaking about knowledge workers, it is very important to communicate the rationale of the decision. We should not only come up with the bottom lines - what is changed and how. We, as managers, are aware of the reasons that brought us to decide upon the change. Even though we are sure that the symptoms are hung out there for all to see, and therefore it is obvious why the change is needed, most times, this is not the case. It is not that we are smarter; we just had the time to think about the reasons, to process, to think about solutions, maybe even several alternatives, and choose one of them, implementing the change. It is important that the employees who did not take part in the process will understand the "Why;" the rationale behind the change. Why is it important for them to understand? To ease implementation. Naturally, people are not enthusiastic about changes; one might say they resist changes. People are comfortable with the status-quo. Explaining the "Why" eases acceptance.

The rationale issue brings me to another recommendation, having to do with channels. We, as human beings, think and act, both upon our rationale, our logic, and upon the emotional, the way we feel. It is important to deal with both channels when managing the change. On the rationale aspect, besides updating the people as to the reasons for the change, we should provide the tools for implementation. On the emotional side, things are more complicated: We should deal with people's fears, both the spoken ones and those that people feel but fear to share. We should enable the employees to participate, mainly in the "how." This gives the employees a good feeling, but the benefit is mainly for the organization: it leaves us with a better plan for change management and with better implementation and chances for success.

It is difficult to manage changes, but we should not avoid them: changes are one of the main factors that leave our organizations relevant, business wise. At the same time, it renews the organization and makes the employees more satisfied in the long run. As much as we fear change, we like to change and renew. Just like our consumers.
I wish us all easy, but successful, changes.

Yours,
   Moria

 Ben, 07/28/2008, 3:35

What you are describing is change within a top-down command and control approach to managing people. This environment by its nature de-motivates employees by treating them with disrespect thus making them highly resistant to change .

In meeting the requirements for change, would it not be better to change the environment such that employees would be agents of change and eagerly embrace necessary change?

To better understand, read the article "Leadership, Good or Bad"
Best regards, Ben
Author "Leading People to be Highly Motivated and Committed"
Ben Simonton

Pat, 07/28/2008, 12:55

Moria

You are right that there are two sides of change - informational and emotional. Consistent communication helps educate the employees about the business needs for the change. With knowledge employees, understanding the reason for the change is important, but these same employees have a strong emotional component to their integration of change.

Most managers feel more comfortable communicating the practical information and hope that the employee will follow easily. They can become frustrated when employees react with their fears about even a simple change.

I worked at a technology company where the leadership assumed that their highly educated employees were professionals and would react appropriately; they were surprised when the employees reacted negatively to the change.

There is so much written around change within organizations. Each of us can see how challenging a specific change can be within our own lives. Even the managers react to the change.

However, we must all give of our best to ensure that change is communicated in many different ways to the employees.

Pat

Tali Helman. 08/20/2008, 20:19

Hi Moria,

I really enjoyed reading your blog on the topic of change management and also the article in the BI newspaper; I learned a lot from both. I wanted to add another small aspect of the matter that I have encountered in the literature: apparently many studies show that organizational elements preceding the change have much influence. This means that when bring about the process of organizational change, the current situation affects the organization as much as how you manage the change. In organizations with a positive organizational climate - namely, trust, a sense of belonging, a sense of information flow, etc. - changes went much more smoothly, and resistance levels decreased, regardless of the change management process and the neutralization of interpersonal differences.

This point might be something to think about when we assess the success of a project in an organization - if we look at including a knowledge management solution in the organizational change management process.

Linda, 08/25/2008, 22:14

Hello Moria,

I liked the idea of preparation that includes elements of cooperation, the kind of partnership that actually shows respect for employees, their knowledge and understanding, when brining them into the process is a significant variable in bringing about the change.

Incidentally, there is another positive yield from this approach - the employee's desire to belong to such an organization

Competing

My brother in-law is a pilot serving in the army. More than once, I have heard stories from him about how he and his fellow pilots, serving in the same squadron, succeeded in fooling the pilots from the other squadron in the same base. One may think that this behavior may suit only youngsters, but there is something deeper to it. This is a competition; the same competition that can be observed between departments in an organization, between units in the army, between scientists in universities.

Competition develops; it urges us on; it inflames our imagination and drives our motivation. No manager suspects that his or her employees do not want to work and will not work if not urged to do so. They are responsible. Managers understand that competition is a partial answer to the endless routine, and that competition can, from time to time, increase production.

Nevertheless, competition and compensation have, besides their benefits, some disadvantages.

The first disadvantage, which I have experienced, has to do with how it is interpreted by the employees. "Don't you trust us," they may ask, "to give the best we can, also without being rewarded ?"
The second disadvantage relates to our difficulty to set the right parameters for rewarding the competition, to our limitations in affecting success. We drive people to compete, sometimes against others, sometimes against themselves, and reward them as to pre-defined desired results. Yet these results depend on various parameters, some external, not dependent on us, no matter how we act. This may not be a problem if someone was rewarded, relying also on luck; nevertheless, when the

opposite occurs, frustration can occur. The more people expect the greater their disappointment.

The third disadvantage has to do with a negative influence while the competition takes place. As reported in many management books, people want to win, and tend to make figures look better, or at least give their subjective interpretation to results. We do not have to turn to extreme examples such as Enron; each one of us has seen many examples of his own.

Another disadvantage has to do with the effect of the competition on the knowledge worker's other activities. These can be neglected while competing. Management focus on a specific issue enables the allocation of fewer resources to other issues, both by the employees and their managers.

And the last disadvantage, which I have experienced, results from most competitions being a zero-sum competition. What does that mean? If one department wins, necessarily, another has to lose. And, since in many cases there are several departments expecting to win, we have more losers than winners. The consequence is that we also do not benefit from this process.

What do I suggest? Preventing competition? Not at all. Here are some recommendations, based on my experience:

Competition that is not zero-sum is preferred. There are two ways to implement this:

A competition in which, every time, a different amount of people win, regarding their own achievements. Every month I draw-up a competition in which an employee is rewarded for his or her achievements. In most cases, one employee wins the glory, but not every time. In some cases, a team is rewarded for their mutual work; in others, more than one employee may win. It all depends on special achievements, not always having to do with results observed at the end of the month. The amount and the definition are not strict. This way, the "good word" reward is never at someone else's expense. If you deserve it, and the manager knows, you will get it, no matter what others did.

Another "good" competition is competition outside the organization. Every organization has another organization with which it competes. People's incentive to be better than the competition, thinking how activities can be performed on a higher level than anyone else, surely brings into the organization all the energies that we experience with internal competition. Let us invest our energies in beating others, not ourselves. Of course, we have to be careful not to cross the lines and not to go overboard. We have to remain dignified, and even more importantly, to be honest and fair. We should not find ourselves nearing the edge, enabling the end to justify unwanted means. Our internal differentiation consolidates us; it makes us a team. This is the rationale of the competition between army units. Fighting the others makes you more connected to your teammates. It really nothing to do with youth, but is just another way to compete, another way to crystallize us, just without the disadvantages of internal competition in the organization.

We just have to be sure we do it right, without crossing any line, without reducing professional quality, without disrupting human behavior.

I hope we succeed.

Yours,
    Moria

 Pat, 10/27/2008, 5:28

Moria
Your two suggestions are good. Having only one winner all the time doesn't necessarily motivate all employees. Yes, it may motivate the top performers, but how do you work with your average performers
I have always felt like a good manager recognizes individuals and team contributions on a regular basis. People want to be recognized and it's that simple. The most ideal is if a strong manager can create some internal competition within each member of their team, helping each

employee stretch, become better than they were. I know they call them goals...but some fun elements can be added into the personal competition . I also like the idea of creating competition with the competitors.

You are right that a manager has to present and balance competition within his/her department.
Thanks for the subject...enjoyed thinking about the value of competition within the workplace.
Pat

Risk management

Albert Einstein said that only those who take risks and go far find out how far they can go. As human beings and managers, we differ in many ways, including our level of caution or our tendency to take risks. The truth be told, we are even more complicated: I can say for myself, and for some people close to me that on some issues we are careful while on others, we take risks. The type of issue - and not only personality - matters.

Whether we wish it or not, we are exposed to risks in work: we start selling something that seems "sure" and profitable, but the market changes; we start developing a project and we have no guarantee that we will finish it on time, within the cost or with the quality we planned; we can't even be sure that we will finish it at all; we work with a staff of employees, and someone decides to leave; we receive a large order for monthly services from a customer (working on an hourly basis), to find out a few months later that the customer does not have the time to work with us and we cannot accomplish anything close to the capacity (and income) we counted on. The list is endless.

Everybody - managers and workers alike - is exposed to risks. But there is a difference: we as managers have to carry the burden. We have to be responsible: responsible as we face the organization, as we face the workers, and as we face ourselves.

I can say for myself that at work I tend not to take risks, as far as I can control. No matter what I do, I know many surprises come with life without my urging and, as I carry the burden also for others, I tend to be cautious. Situations in which I may take risks are those where the main one to lose is me and not the employees or customers. I was always taught that with risks come opportunities and chances for success, but I hesitate to risk other people. That is why I am not built to manage a start-up; there you must think risk-wise.

Yet there always are and will be risks. Here are some tips I can share from my own experience:

First, scatter the risks; do not put all your eggs in one basket. Prefer several small customers together with one big one. I remember when I was a young girl I was exposed to a business that was dependent on one large customer. I remember the day when the connection with this customer came to an end. When I set up a business, ten years ago, and landed my first large customer, it implied a significant growth of my company (from two to five employees). That was the day when I stopped sleeping at night. I started seeking other customers; I was almost in a panic. It took time, almost too much time, until I stabilized another large activity of the same dimensions. The same month, the first big customer collapsed and our work there almost vanished. It is very tempting to work with a significant customer, but we should be sure that this customer does not exceed 50% of our income. If the company grows larger, the percentage even has to decrease.

The same goes for other risks: It is better to have a few small projects than one large one, several products and not one, etc. Take a look at what is happening, for example, with the Crocs Company (which sold shoes, until people got tired of them, with no real reason at all).

The risks should be managed, but do not over-manage them. We must make priorities regarding the risks we manage and those we leave out. We must remember that we want to manage and work, not only manage risks about work. We have to decide what on the right frequency for managing these risks. As a rule of thumb, I would say that once a month is a good ratio, but if we are managing a crisis, we manage the risks on a daily basis, or even several times a day, if necessary.

It is important to decide how to manage the risk. As much as it sounds difficult, data and information should be collected, wherever possible, and used in order to aid managing the risk. Relying on facts and data will help us be more objective and decrease the risk. Sometimes we think it is not worth seeking, as we probably will not find information or data that will help us anyhow. Yet it is worthwhile trying.

Business Intelligence is based on decision support information of three types: Monitoring (what is happening), Analyzing (why did things happen) and Planning (what can happen in the future). One of the main targets of planning is risk management of the future. It turns out that most of the best performance organizations manage their risks, and do so using Business Intelligence (BI).

However, as we all know, life is more than quantified numbers. It consists of many qualified, intangible facts and assumptions. We have to use other management mechanisms, over and above the BI ones, in order to decide upon the level of the risk (how likely is it to occur); upon its severity (if it indeed occurs); and upon ways of preventing the risk or minimizing its impact.

What do I do?

I try hearing other people, who naturally see reality from different points of view.

Wherever possible, I consult someone external, not emotionally involved, who can see the big picture and maybe enlighten me with new understanding;

Finally yet importantly, I recommend not hesitating. At the end of the day, we as managers have to decide to cut things down. It is our decision as it is our responsibility.

We will fail. I fail in some risks I take, or am forced to manage (because of external influences). Nevertheless, with some risks I do succeed.

At these times, I try to remember that, after all, only those who take risks and go far, find out how far they can go.

I wish us all success wherever we are and specifically success in managing our risks and failing less.

Yours,
Moria

Empowerment

I admit that the first time that I encountered the concept of empowerment was five years ago. I did not previously recognize the term. I remember that we were working on a project for some customer in the educational sector. If I try to analyze the customer's organization, without too much generalization, I can say that they were afraid of computers. Some of them were terrified. Building a website and knowledge sharing was a very different process than we recognized and had experienced in other places. As part of trying to make things easier for them, we used many techniques; for example, we left many blank areas on each page so that it would look less threatening. In addition, all graphic art was planned accordingly.

On the contrary, the home page of this website included many terms describing the main values of the organization. It included terms such as democracy, autonomy, activism, enrichment and more. Of course, empowerment was one of the values.

The truth be told I did not relate to those ideas at all; it seemed to me as if the ideas were taken from the ivory tower and were not borne out in our day-to-day conception. I wondered about the polarity of my reflection on those ideas versus my reflections on computers and their use as a sharing tool. I admit that I misunderstood the importance of those ideas, being a person that defines herself as rational and practical.

I grew up; I have changed. Also today, I try to rely on the conception of practice; yet I have learned the influence of empowerment and its capability.

Dr. Elisheva Sadan defines empowerment as a process with an impact that passes from a situation of helplessness, to a situation of relative control over life, fate and surroundings. This shift can be expressed by

94

improving the sense of one's capability to control or by improving the real capability to set in motion this control.

The original meaning of the idea is a way of granting power of attorney - approval to work in the name of the company - a kind of delegation of authority granted to one in the social plane. There are four categories of empowerment: individual, community based, cooperative and professional. What is not surprising, and of course most positive, is that empowerment in one category usually affects the other categories, improving them too.

In my terminology, empowerment is a process of development; whether individual, community, collective or professional, it involves strengthening and handing over abilities and skills so that the empowered person can utilize his or her potential in different realms.

How is empowerment relevant to us as managers?

One of the main roles we have as managers, as I see it, is to empower the managers on the scale below us and empower the employees. I personally dedicate a main percentage of my time, management efforts and resources to this activity. Naturally, I concentrate mostly on professional empowerment, about which I intend to write and share in this post. As you might have already gathered, I did not always deal with professional empowerment with this same intensity. I assume that in my first years as a manager I felt the need to be on the front stage. I concentrated on guiding workers and advancing their skills, but I thought that as a manager I needed to be in front of them. I thought that the right way to lead them forward was by giving a good example and shouting "after me."

It is hard to invest hours, time and energy in empowerment. The goal of most of organizations is to create or to provide service. We always have missions to complete; we always have activities regarding a product, service or customer. Usually, their due date is yesterday (or in good cases, tomorrow). To stop in order to invest in empowerment is not a simple challenge. It is so too easy to postpone the important issues as we are confronted by the urgent ones.

How do I reduce the chances this will happen?

In two ways:
First, I remind myself repeatedly of the importance of staff empowerment.
Second, I nominate workers to be responsible for empowerment, and define resources for doing so (mainly time). This is not enough to cover all the aspects of empowerment, but it is enough to constantly and significantly advance them.

I know that it is fashionable today to talk about talent management - locating a small percentage of workers with exceptional potential and investing more in their empowerment. I am in favor of the opposite method: empowerment of all workers. From my point of view they are all talented. It is clear to me that since the resources are always limited, it means less investment in each one.
As I see it, there is a moral statement here about my faith in each one of my workers; there is a statement here about my faith in us as an organization. We hired talented people. They are all talented. They all have potential to be even more talented. That is what empowerment is about.

It is very important to communicate to the workers how important it is to us to empower them, and how important it is to us that they actually will be empowered.

There are two aspects here:
The first one is to encourage the workers to grow; to give them the legitimization to take over new territory at their work.

The second is a message to workers that we believe that they have a great potential. A person's belief in him/herself is the key to the success of his or her empowerment.

Over and above the formal empowerment frame, it is worthwhile to take advantage of opportunities that enable us to strengthen empowerment.
Recently I was ill. I was absent from work for a long time. It is unfortunate, but it was an excellent opportunity to empower workers and managers. My absence from the office gave the junior managers more place to express themselves in different terms, where in other circumstances I would have been involved. A simple example is lecturing in conferences. Organizers of conferences often prefer the senior person, and naturally I am the one invited to lecture and present. My absence required others' participation in my stead; suddenly they became known in their seniority. They moved to the front stage.

In my first years as a manager, I thought that to be a manager meant being on the front stage, setting good examples and seeing that people follow me. Today I know that it is right to begin in this way, but the wisdom is in the next stage - to be wise enough to move aside or even to the back, and concentrate on removing all obstacles, allowing the managers and the workers below me to run in the lead.
This is the essence of empowerment. Today I know that it is more difficult to lead when you are behind, but in that way you get much further.

Yours
   Moria

Planning

A few weeks ago, I was invited to a big event. Many ceremonies are taking place around the country, as Israel is currently celebrating 60 years of independence. This event was a military one, aimed at saluting a large group of technical people. Usually those people are in the shadow, servicing others. Therefore the uniqueness of this event lay in placing them in the spotlight and thanking them for their significant activity that contributes to the complete success and security.

Thousands of people were invited to the event and most of them did show up. Unfortunately, an hour before the ceremony started, somewhere else in Israel, two soldiers were killed in a training accident. After waiting a while, the event was canceled. Five thousand people were sent back home with no party. We are a family, the commander said, explaining the cancellation, after every one had already arrived. A family in good times and in sad times. Today is one of the sad times. We cannot celebrate.

Can we plan anything? Is there any meaning to planning? I am sure that the brigadier general that set the event in motion, and worked diligently on turning it into reality for six months did not imagine that the event would end the way it did. I am convinced that the families of the killed soldiers, that sent their beloved ones to another day of operations, did not think that they would never see them again.

Even when we deal with less important events, we plan and not always successfully stick to the original plan. In the beginning of my professional path, as a consultant, I remember that I received a purchase order from a client, after several months of working on the lead. Two weeks later, the company was merged with some other company. I was left with an order in my hand, yet with an organization in flux, an organization unable to execute the activity. The button line: zero revenue.

I have many more examples. We plan, and agree on some things with an employee, customer or a partner, but reality is stronger than any plan. Time is an issue - something else is urgent and our activity is postponed; managers are replaced and our plan is canceled. In some cases, an activity starts and an external constraint prevents its completion. The list of reasons why plans are not fulfilled is very long.

Should we conclude that we should not plan? Or shall we deal with changes affecting our plans?

I will start from the ending point. In "Alice in wonderland" Alice asks the cat, as she reaches the intersection: "Which way I should choose?" "Where do you want to get to?" She was asked. "I don't know." "If so," the cat replied, "Any road will lead you there."

We need to plan. Planning serves to define the direction in which we want to go; designing defines the long-term direction, as well as the intermediate stations (the tasks) that will help us get there.

Planning assists us in getting much further.

Planning assists us in estimating the required sources (time, expense and other sources).

Moreover, planning assists us in noticing the risks, so that we can prepare ourselves in the best way possible.

Yet planning is only an introduction to life, and therefore may be considered as a baseline for changes. I do believe that we should not stick to the original plan in every case and never give up. It is necessary to work according to a plan, but also to know when this plan turns to be only a plan and not anything beyond.

We should be careful not to turn the planning and the work plans into a target rather than an aid. I have often seen an over emphasis on plans and their details: repeated updating, drawing all management attention to the planning. We are limited in our ability to dedicate management resources to too many simultaneous tasks. We need to remember that the goal of a work plan is to help us; the plan is not the project or the activity itself. It is possible that the best solution, in case of a need to change, is only a new layout rather than dismantling the entire work plan. In other cases, it is possible that the solution includes introducing changes to a work plan without getting into details. It is possible that we, as managers, can ensure a full work plan, but will guide an employee below us to deal with the details. There are a wide range of solutions. All we have to do is decide that we are willing to compromise. The rest is simple.

Primarily, however, we need to know not under any circumstance to trust the planning as a promise. You are not a start up or a futuristic project of R&D? So do not act as if you are. If there is a certain forecast of revenue, do not spend it all in advance, as if the excels are reality. Not as a regular expense and not as an investment. Wait until you see the revenues in your bank account. My recommendation is to remember the difference between plans and reality.

I have learned, reading Goldratt's management theories, an interesting perception: in any work plan, we save reserves for time of crisis. Reserves of time, reserves of money. In actual life, we burn them all, even if there is no major problem standing in the way. There is more time left? Let us add more features and capabilities to the built appliance, or invest more in the finish. There is money? We use more equipment and parts and, as before, no reserves are left.

The situation resembles our attitude to our personal salary: If it becomes higher, most of us get used to higher consumption. We fit ourselves to the existing resources.

Planning triggers resource consumption, even if the resources were planned for a rainy day.

How can we improve our planning? Goldratt suggests saving all the reserves in a special bank, leaving it in a separate section, the "reserves" section. We will allow its use only when there is a real problem and additional resources are truly required. That way, we will ensure that the work plan will converge, usually sticking closer to the average need without using part or all of the reserves. Those stay until the end in the separate section. It is too easy to spend them, and this technique helps manage the reserves and controls their use.

I make efforts to build my work plan this way: minimal, but with flexibility. It saves both me and the customer money.

Twentieth century management has made us a bit technocratic, with all its management control tools. In the 21st century, I believe, we must remember that we have to be much more flexible and creative in many aspects - even in planning and in work plans.

Yours,
   Moria

 # Words

"Life and death are in the power of the tongue," said King Solomon in the Bible (Proverbs 18:21). Sages of Blessed Memory added: "silence is a fence for wisdom." Speaking is not always the right thing to do. Using words does not add in all cases.

Words are no doubt significant. They always have been. However, it seems that when it comes to work, the power of words becomes even greater. Why is this so? For two reasons:

Firstly, in the reality that existed one hundred years ago, the employee had less interaction with his/her manager. Therefore, also if words were powerful, there were fewer opportunities for using them in employee-manager communication. Secondly, the relationship between the manager and the employee has in recent years become symmetrical in some ways and in others not. This lack of balance causes the written or spoken word to have much more influence. I will explain:

Today, employment is symmetrical. This issue has been dealt in previous posts, but I wish to return to it and explain its consequences on the use of words. In the past, a place to work was a choice for life. Today, people regularly move on every few years, changing their employment. The initiative for such a change could come from the manager, but could also come from the worker. This is the symmetry. If, as a manager, you have said something negative to an employee, or even if you have been understood in that way, the employee can easily remember and become angry and bitter. These feelings can be translated, over time, to people not wishing to stay in a place of work. It is not easy to know about such things. As in other aspects of life, such relationships are easier to ruin than to fix. In the former situation, also if such feelings would exist, their influence on the employee's remaining at his/her workplace was minimal. As employees knew that they were staying in the same job for many years, they knew how to ignore, how not to take every issue and blow it

102

up. This resembles the relationship of a married couple. We know that the relationship is important; we know we want it to last. So we learn, as adults, not to get insulted by everything the other says. It is obvious that two grown people cannot see everything in the same way, yet it is not worth breaking one's heart over. The fact that we see a specific place of work as a stage only eases its breaking.

Yet there is an asymmetrical part of the manager-employee relationship that always was and is here to stay: The word of a manager has more power. It has more influence. It flies further.

The combination of these two factors, the symmetric and the asymmetric, makes life unbalanced. It makes the power of the word more significant.

I have learnt a few things along the way, some of them, the hard way:

Beware of what you write to your employees. Especially when using email. Formal documents are in most cases professional, and rarely serve as part of the communication between a manager and his or her employee. When we speak with our employee face to face, we see them, hear them and sense them. It is easier to fix mistakes if we failed in choosing our words. If we write a mail, on the other hand, backing off and rephrasing is much more complicated. Emails tend to be one dimensional, and the employee's impression is not supported by our facial expression, by the tone we use when we speak and by all our body language, which are, as researchers claim, the main part of what is understood in any message.

The use of Email in the 21st century flattens the organization in some aspects and should be considered as a blessing, yet it has potential faults as well. The flattening enables a channel of communication between various levels in the organization, communication that does not exist in other channels. The impact of every written word empowers, as it is not supported by the frame of all other accompanying channels, leaving the communication mainly in one channel, with only one dimension. Therefore, be careful! Even though it is tempting to write in a short and straightforward manner, when writing Emails, consider every word and express your decision in more than one way. That way, the chances of misunderstanding decrease. Of course, and this we should memorize time after time, many issues should not be dealt with by mail at all.

When you talk, and even more important, when you write, consider avoiding criticizing together with giving compliments. We should keep in mind, as managers, that in many cases the compliment becomes transparent. Nobody notices it, even if it was the major part of the message. It does not matter if the compliment precedes the criticism or succeeds it. I have learnt over and over again that people are selective in what they decide to catch. What do I recommend? Deciding what is most important in each case, and sticking to it, without adding the other part; or, taking the risk that some part of the message will be disregarded.

This is the place, before continuing, for an important tip. It is somehow natural for us to criticize, and less natural to appreciate and value good performance. Appreciate your employees! When someone does a good job, do not treat it as obvious. Tell him or her what you think or, even better, write it. Even a short mail will do the job. It does not cost, but it is worth a lot. You would not believe as how much our employees yearn to hear something good from us, how important it is to them. They deserve it, so give it! Say something good.

However, do not exaggerate. Write and say only the truth. The words we use and their value are subjective. If we re-use the term "excellent" too much, for example, its value, to the listener, will decrease drastically. If we do not give a compliment every day, about every thing, when we do compliment, its value is amazingly high. That way, it is also easy for us to give the compliment, to say a good word, as we feel inside our hearts, that the people deserve it, that it is significant.

One last thing: when we want to pass an important message, it is best do so three times. Use more than one mail, or use more than one communication channel. We were born that way as people. In order not only to hear but also to listen; not only to read, but also for the heart and mind to understand, we must return and say these things repeatedly.

Maybe, not in all situations, "life and death are in the power of the tongue," but in all cases, words are truly significant. For better and for worse.
On that, Sages of Blessed Memory said: "Wise people, beware what you say".

Yours,
   Moria

Motivation

Shaye Feinbaum, a well-known Israeli football coach, once explained to reporters: "People say I am a 'motivator;' that means someone who injects motivation into his players."

No doubt, in every profession, from football and to teaching, through manufacturing, medicine and art, the worker's motivation is an essential factor of his or her productivity. No doubt, too that motivation cannot be purchased by any check signed by a manager.

There are many theories that speak about motivation that triggers activity and, hopefully, assists in achieving desired goals. Two of the more famous of these are Maslow's hierarchy of needs theory and John Adam's equity theory. Maslow defined a pyramid of needs, starting with physiological needs, through safety needs, love/belonging needs, esteem needs and to self-actualization needs. The individual's behavior is influenced by all. In order to achieve motivation, we should fulfill all five levels of the individual's needs. The lowest level of unfulfilled needs will be the one that blocks the individual's motivation. For example, if an individual does not feel safe in his/her place of work, then while s/he may be thoroughly respected (esteem level), s/he will not feel motivated. And vice versa. The more we invest in supplying the necessities of the individual, on more levels, our chances of gaining the motivation of our worker will rise.

Adams speaks about another aspect affecting worker's motivation: equity. Individuals want fair treatment. Fair is defined by comparing what the person invests in the organization to what s/he receives. Fairness is also defined by comparing what the specific person receives as compared to what other colleagues receive, those near (in the same team / place of work) and those further defined (working in the same profession /friends,

106

etc.). The Adams theory enables us to better implement Maslow's hierarchy of needs theory. If workers feel that what they receive is relatively fair, even if we provide partial answers to their needs, these may be enough for triggering motivation. Even if the business is experiencing difficulties (economical or others), what is important is the relative answer we give to the individual rather than the absolute one.

Above all these wise and important theories, I use various tools in order to motivate people:
First, I understand that there cannot be a uniform level of motivation for all employees and for each employee every day of the year. Motivation is triggered also by character, and people are different from one another. Motivation is also influenced by external factors, factors that we cannot control: coming angry to work, someone in the family sick, separation, etc. We have to be empathic to our employees and compare each one of them only to him/herself and to no one else. If we feel motivation decreases, we should give it place, and pay attention so as to learn if it is an external passing problem, or a sign that there is a motivation problem of the employee.

On the individual level:
I try to delegate authority. When a person knows that s/he is trusted, motivation increases. Of course, we have to prevent them from feeling like "suckers" or helpless. Delegating authority must be accompanied with guidance, and should be conducted in an atmosphere of open mindedness and not abuse.
I try to challenge my people. Challenges promote motivation;
I try to match part of the assignments to things that I know the worker relates to or likes to do. I try to highlight these aspects in existing activities;
Moreover, I try to respect and thank. Cherishing people for successful activities and good results is the fuel for motivation in the next activity.

On the personal level, I try, as much as possible, to show people how motivated I am. I try to be a good example, to serve as a role model. If we, as managers, are motivated, and if we are out there with a sparkle in our eyes, we enhance the chances of our workers being motivated; the opposite is true too.

On the organizational level, two related tips:
First, a good organizational climate; and second, share what is going on with the employees.
There are only few things better than causing our employees to want to come to work every morning, smiling and motivated to work. In my company, a few moths ago, we held our yearly satisfaction review. Naturally, the people included criticism, and naturally, even though the "big picture" was positive, these comments left me sad. The day after we published the results, one of the employees knocked on my door. He said: "I want you to know, that even though people included less favorable comments too, I come to work every day smiling; I like to come to work and I am certainly not the only one that feels that way." We cannot always have people say only good things and thank us. People tend to want better, and that is a good thing, because it makes the organization better. Yet we have to remember to ensure that the climate is good and that the atmosphere is positive. We have to ensure that our employees are happy to work in our organization, and happy to start their day with us.

What does this have to do with sharing with the employees? Employees that share in what is happening feel more safe and less threatened (rumors are a recipe for trouble) and feel a greater sense of belonging to the organization. Safety and belonging drive motivation. Did we mention, by any chance, Maslow's hierarchy of needs theory?

Yours,
    Moria

2008-11-13 14:15

 # A good manager

I have been writing this blog now for over a year, every time looking at another aspect, another issue concerning management, trying to highlight it for myself and for the readers. Doing so, I find myself wondering: if we collect all the written literature, here, in other blogs and all over the web, in hundreds and thousands of management books, it seems as if the list of skills required for being what is called a "good manager" is endless.

I feel as if anyone who wishes to fulfill this list and become a good manager should be a superman; some virtuoso that is A and B and C, and so on.

It is important, I believe, to discuss the issue, for two complementary reasons:

The first, as a tool for examining myself, seeking where I should focus my efforts for improvement; the second, in order to better choose subordinate managers and help them better develop so they best manage their employees.

If I would have to choose five and only five skills of a good manager, I believe I would choose the following:

A manager is a person who knows to make decisions. To listen, to understand, to ask; to agree, to disagree. But at the end of the day- to make a decision. And to know that I am responsible and not later blame my partners, my employees, my customers and certainly not the weather. To make decisions and be responsible for them.

A manager is a person who knows how to motivate people. Motivate people to act; motivate people to act effectively; motivate people to work with a sparkle in their eyes and enthusiasm in their hearts. Motivating people is important in a stable work environment, but all the more critical in the changing market we are experiencing now in the 21st century. The changing market causes us to check and recheck our decisions, to refine or even change them due to the circumstances, and to motivate people to act upon these changes.

A manager is a person with a presence; a person whom others actually want to listen to and to follow.

A manager is a person who acts. This has several aspects: Acts - does not find it undignified to work and even to perform some dirty work. Acts - is connected to the field and continues to deal, though less, with the professional discipline in which the company specializes. Acts - analyzes the past and brings in the future.

A good manager is somewhat different. Creative, innovative, knows how to think out-of-the-box, sometimes thinking differently to others. Your employees do not expect you to think exactly as they do; the organization needs you to think somewhat differently in order to burst forward and lead. Moreover, you have to find the right way to proceed, and not always the trivial one. You have to be willing to take risks and know that sometimes you will pay for taking them.

A good manager is a person. Empathetic, attentive, laughing sometimes, other times angry. Also, having weaknesses. Externalize the person you are.

Some readers may ask: Does humanity (us being people) compensate for professionalism, for the skill of, for example, making decisions? The answer is, without a doubt, no. Being human, and even externalizing it, resembles the attitude to the zero digit. A zero, if it comes before a number (01, 079, 013456) adds nothing. However, a zero digit added after a number (10,790, 134560) adds a magnitude. It multiplies by factor 10. I believe that humanity acts in a similar way: Without the other skills, it is useless. When it comes above them, it's what makes the difference.

Be human. Teach your employees whom you manage to do the same.

If I succeed in sticking even only to this list of skills, I hope and believe that I can be in a situation where I navigate the ship, at the right speed, with smiling sailors on deck.

I surely try.

Yours,
  Moria

 Anonymous, 11/27/2008, 23:06

Hi,

One key measure of effective managers lies in their ability to get things done through other people -- a prime ingredient for success.

Conflicts

Conflicts are natural: it is natural that different people will have different opinions; it is natural that different people will have different agendas that they wish to promote. Therefore it is natural that conflicts will take place.

We all, also I, tend to refer to conflicts negatively. Nevertheless, as our world is complicated, we must notice that there are also positive results caused by conflicts (and I wish to thank the leading and control guide and the free library of management):

Conflicts help to sharpen and bring some issues to our awareness;

Conflicts drive people to act upon their truth;

Conflicts trigger organizational and personal energy; if channeled correctly, it leverages us.

Yet, if conflicts are not handled and managed, we lose control, and the conflicts can damage both the activities as well as the organization's morality.

Here are several factors that can cause higher level conflicts in organizations:

- Competitive atmosphere in the office.
  Encourages conflicts.
- Period of uncertainty (low level of security).
  Enables conflicts' eruption, caused by the high level of tension.
- Unclear designation of job definitions and overlapping between jobs.
  Causes people to interfere in each other's jobs and, sooner or later, drives many conflicts.
- Low level of communication between people

Does not cause conflicts directly, but surely enables them, as when any suspicion exists, it takes an unwanted direction if not clarified fast enough.

As best as you can, examine this list and see how you can deal with it. Prevention is always far better than dealing with an existing problem.

Many people speak about finding a win-win solution as a way of resolving conflicts. Contradicted opinions often come from the personal interests of those holding them, but analysis of the interests can build a new shared decision that does not oppose (or only opposes a little) each side's interests. The idea of mediation is based significantly on this concept. What do I think? A great idea, but surely no "magic maker" as people may tend to believe. Sometimes it resolves the conflict, sometimes partially, and sometimes it does not do the job. In some cases the conflict is deep-seated and win-win solutions do not exist.

Of course, speaking to each other helps to handle every conflict and can be a very effective tool. A tool for communication, a tool for being attentive, a tool for understanding differences, and even... a tool for venting. It's simple, but it works.
And, of course, preventing a conflict from being loudly expressed can help, as well as preventing blaming and preventing turning the conversation from issues to people. These are trivial, yet always correct and surely do their job.

Two tips, I found, that help me:
First, willingness to concede and to give up on part of the issues that I think are right, not because I am convinced that I made a mistake, but as part of showing the person with whom I am in a conflict that I am trying to find a way to approach him or her. People act in reciprocity. If we move closer to them, in many cases, they will move closer to us. Again, simple, but effective. In this way the conflict can shrink and may be handled.

A second tip that helps me: respecting the other person and opinion, even if I disagree, and even if I do not resolve the conflict itself. I disagree with one of my workers as to how a certain issue should be handled. I tried, two years ago, to give up and let that person handle a big project according to her way. I won't say that there were not good aspects and good results. Yet, as I believed in the first place, there were aspects that I liked less. Now, when a similar project with the same issue is again to be handled, I have decided to lead it my way. But I do it, both then and now, while respecting the opposite opinion and the person holding it. I am not trying to state that there is no conflict; there certainly is and we live with it. Not even badly, I believe.

As I said at the beginning of my post, life is complicated. Understanding the complexity and that we have to live and strive, not always resolving every issue and not always having win-win solutions, decreases part of the frustration, and assists us in living with conflicts. Maybe it even weakens some of them.

I wish us all a pleasant life and, if possible, good energy-driving conflicts, and not annoying ones.

Yours,
  Moria

2008-12-10 20:19

 # Measurement

A known saying among management people speaks about measurement: Whatever cannot be measured cannot be managed.

The importance of measuring is obvious.

Measurement enables us, first of all, to examine if an activity was successful. We measure whether we succeeded in achieving targets defined in advance. As our world is not just black and white, measurement deals not only with examining if we reached targets, but also how close we came.

Measurement, however, has several additional advantages above the measurement of success and achievement of targets:

Measuring is our way to examine the path we have chosen in order to help ourselves refine the path and learn how to proceed, instead of waiting for the end and possibly even failing. Early measurement can point out ways to fix problems before they grow large, and can show us the way for improvement. Measurement here is defined by methods and techniques, and not only by results.

Measuring is our way, as we move along, of identifying trends and changes that pass nearby, without us noticing them otherwise.

Measuring is our proof to authorities or customers, external and internal, that we act as declared.

Measurement is a positive step. It takes us forward and is a base for comparison.

Yet a few points should be made, clarifying that the essence of measurement and the way it is obtained are far more complicated than we would like them to be:

Albert Einstein said: "Everything that can be counted does not necessarily count; everything that counts cannot necessarily be counted..."
What can we learn from this sentence?
We have to be cautious not to search for the coin under the street lamp. Too many times we rush to measure, ending up with a set of indicators and measurements that measure what is simple, rather than what is important. Start with targets and measure the important factors regarding these targets; do not yield for the easy way.

More complexity derives from the ease of measuring results, but the relative difficulty of segregating the various factors of the result and understanding how much our activity contributed to this result. For example, a successful activity was held by the company, yielding positive business results, and we decided to reward all employees involved. A month later, we measure the employees' satisfaction and find it high. How can we know, from the satisfaction measurement only, whether satisfaction is triggered by the bonus or maybe by the professional success they were part of? Moreover, the opposite can happen too: we can proceed successfully, yet an external event, such as the economic crisis we are experiencing now, will contribute to negative business results. It is possible that had we not held the company activities, results would be worse; but we really cannot know - segregating is difficult. This complexity is one of the reasons that drive qualitative measurement. Qualitative measurement deals with the impression created: what impression did people get from the activities held? To what point did the activity contribute to success? To what point was it successful, despite ultimate failure? In most cases, people are intelligent enough to segregate factors and provide a reliable answer.

Complexity derives also from the measures and indicators that we set. Naturally, we as people are subjective, and our assessment differs from that of our colleagues. If they would run the activity, possibly we would have a different list of measurements, and a different list of results yielding. This challenge is magnified when we evaluate people, rather than activities. A person who may think he is friendly and a teammate might be considered from his/her manager's viewpoint as a soloist. And this is only one example among many.

A last tip regarding measurement while managing people and activities:
Measure values at least as much as measuring results. Values represent the strategy by which we wish to act. If these are correct, and people work by them, then we are on the right track.

After all this, I wish to end with a proverb. This time, not a quote from Albert Einstein, rather a old Indian saying: "You can measure how deep the well is, but you cannot measure the deepness of the heart."
The people and their hearts are as least as important as the activities (the well).
Let us measure; however, let us remember and cherish the deepness of the heart.

Yours,
    Moria

Atul, 12/10/ 2008, 8:27 PM

Excellent points you have raised here ... to add, in a lot of scenarios, its just not possible to measure things which are relevant, so we opt for proxy measures, which may or may not be reliable indicators.

But I think you have brought out quite well the whole idea of measurement, and the way we ought to look at it.

Tradition

As a Jewish Israeli child brought up in the US, I remember back at home the same songs played repeatedly on my parents' gramophone. One of the songs I remember clearly is "Tradition" from "Fiddler on the Roof." The musical is a personal story in a world of traditions, dating to the beginning of the 20th century in Russia: the Jewish tradition, the class status tradition ("If I were a rich man"), the tradition that grants different rights and authorities to genders, and the tradition of matchmakers, a tradition that Tzirel, the fiddler's daughter, tries to break.

The song "Tradition" returns to me, again and again, and leaves me with nostalgia and a good feeling. Yet, if I stop and listen to the words, I cannot see even one sentence that I identify with. The issue presents an internal conflict: On the one hand, tradition produces feelings of a warm and friendly environment; on the other hand, as the Etnix band have sung: "tradition is the enemy of advancement and progress."

What is the place of tradition in organizations? Is it right to nurture it and how should this be done?

These days I am celebrating ten years of running my company. A decade. I have gone through a long journey and yet it went by so quickly, and seems rather short. Again, the conflict arises:

On one hand, there is so much yet to do. We came here to work, innovate, earn and bring about a change. Why look at the past? Why spend time and effort on traditions and memories that take us back? How can it help? On the other hand, I feel, both as a manager and as a person, that tradition and memories do have their place in the organization and should be honored rather than swept out.

Tradition has clear advantages: it enables people to strengthen their feelings of belonging, of feeling part of the organization in another dimension - not only part of some office; not only tools and methodologies; and even not only values. Tradition is something shared that passes in the air very simply. It makes us feel better. It makes us feel as if we belong to something greater.

Tradition also crystallizes.

Tradition, I hope, is another factor that makes people prefer to stay in the organization and not look for other opportunities outside it. Tradition makes people in the organization better deal with daily difficulties (and we have no choice, difficulties always exist). Tradition makes them feel better.

Tradition.

How does this line up with "the enemy of advancement and progress?" We, as human beings, probably need both: both tradition and revival; both anchors and stability together with the ability to change; both the feelings that tradition produces together with the legitimization to create and fly high and far.

The challenge of tradition, therefore, is more complicated. It should enable, but not block; it should be part of the background, but should not gain control. We have to remember that few are the organizations that survive due to tradition only.

How do we produce tradition in the organization? I will start at the bottom line: money is not the main issue here. One cannot order tradition, pay for it, and check it off. One must invest. Invest and be consistent. And after all these - wait. Time is an important element when speaking about tradition.

What and how? Here are several factors that produce and nurture tradition:

Holidays. Naama, one of my junior managers, taught me and insisted repeatedly, until I understood and assimilated, that every holiday must be celebrated. I always came with a pragmatic attitude that every company meeting, and every minute in it, should be utilized: more methodologies, more teaching people, more professionalism. Tradition is important, she always reminded me: it is important to eat an apple with honey together before the Jewish New Year, and we must together finish eating together all the "Hametz" (leaven) before Passover. From year to year, the place of tradition in the company, based on celebrating Jewish events, grows greater. From two celebrations a year, we began celebrating more holidays, and in between, we find new opportunities for additional and varied celebrations.

Tradition can also be nurtured through simple ceremonies and customs that are repeated from time to time. The ritual produces the tradition. Smoking breaks produces tradition (in this case, tradition has also disadvantages). Tradition evolves through our monthly ritual of giving, every month, a symbolic prize for something special that someone did during the past month. Tradition evolves only because it is done consistently every month, for years.

Tradition evolves through building new memories together and speaking about existing memories. We see to it that on every company trip or event we take pictures (so easy nowadays), and in the last years this became even more sophisticated as we make a clip after each event. It is much more pleasant to remember, and much easier too. In relevant events, we turn back to the past and share the memories. Share, with those who took part in past events, and share and explain to those who were not there yet. Share through stories, through pictures, through feelings. Build and strengthen the tradition.

These days I am celebrating ten years of running my company. I can surely say that we have produced a company tradition. A tradition inside the company and a tradition in larger groups, both with our customers and with the Israeli Knowledge Management community. We have come a long way, but I do hope that the main path is still before us. We hope we smartly combine tradition and advancement. We hope to continue marching at the right pace, and make others follow. We hope to produce many more (good) traditions that make all feel belonging, feel sharing and feel good.

Sorry for being so sentimental today. I promise to return to myself in the next posts.

Yours,
　Moria

 Nurit Weisberg, 01/09/2009, 00:14

Greetings Moria,

As one who deals with cross-cultural work and with the connections between ancient traditions and present reality, I would like to offer another observation about the importance of tradition. The existence of a tradition is necessary in order to implement changes; in its absence the change has no base to hold to, and the organization like "society" must use what exists in order to absorb the new. Berl Katznelson, described this well when he said:

"A new and creating generation does not relegate to the junkyard the legacy of generations. It examines and checks, expands and distances. There is the generation that clings to tradition and adds to it; and there is one that goes down to the junkyard, revealing what was forgotten, polishing off the rust and regenerating ancient tradition, which is able to feed the soul of the new generation. "

Organizational structure

Henri Fayol, a French management theoretician, already in 1916, defined fourteen management principles that have become a well-known list for all managers. Among the items on the list are principles of rewarding, the management chain, the fraternity of the group, and more. One of these principles, discussed also by many other management theoreticians, is the principle that every employee has one manager in charge of him. This sounds like a very natural principle: multiplicity of managers for a single employee can confuse him/her, can decrease efficiency (caused by holes in time when each manager is partially in charge) and can raise organizational political problems when conflicts develop. The list of potential problems is long, and it is reasonable, therefore, that for many years organizations were based on a hierarchical structure.

In the past years, however, new needs have developed, raising questions about the correctness and suitability of the classical hierarchical organization structure for all purposes and for all circumstances. That many workers are knowledge workers is an important parameter influencing both on needs and the implacable solutions.
Knowledge workers are workers whose knowledge plays a significant role in their activities. Developing the knowledge is a central component of their professionalism.

How does such a worker learn and develop his/her knowledge? Knowledge develops through personal experience, through team working, and by having a guiding manager pushing one forward.
Personal experience exists independent of the organizational structure. If we want to leverage this, it is preferable that the experience is diverse.
Working in teams enables us to learn from our colleagues who may have different education, skills and characteristics. The organizational structure influences the teams to which each employee is assigned.

122

The manager and his/her ability to guide are surely influenced by the organizational structure.

All three are intensified when the organizational structure is not hierarchical, when the worker has an opportunity for more diverse activities, taking part in several teams (each including different people) and working with several managers, each manager adding his/her observation.

Based on these, several years ago, I set up a heterarchical organizational structure in the company that I manage. The Internet defines a heterarchical organizational structure as a form of organization resembling a network or fishnet, where authority is determined by knowledge and function. Such a structure resembles the matrix known organizational structure (also called "M-form"), but is rather loose. It is a network, but not as strict as the classical matrix that has employees assigned to two well-defined dimensions of managers. I have adopted this structure, and while it may seem like cognitive dissonance, I see its advantages every day.

The managers in my company each have a different combination of education, experience, skills and character, all relevant to the profession in which we specialize. In each project, we decide ad-hoc which manager will lead and who will be included in the work team.. We will always recommend part time participation, enabling the team workers to continue their participation in other projects at the same time.

In practice, this project assignment method leads to a situation in which every employee experiences diverse activities, is assigned to several teams, in which every time s/he learns and shares knowledge with different people. Furthermore, the professional manager varies from project to project, and the employee benefits learning from the experience of various managers (usually more senior).

Six months after I set up this organizational structure, I found out its name (the heterarchical organizational structure) and learned that a researcher, named Hedlund, wrote an article, already in 1994, claiming that knowledge based units, like R&D, should be managed according to this structure. Hedlund defined principles for heterarchical management, and coined this method "the N-FORM," N standing for novelty, or new. The novelty of this model compared the classical M-FORM, is:

    a. Combination of issues and people in the N-FORM, compared to defined distribution in the M-FORM.

    b. Temporary constellations of people and units in the N-FORM, instead of stable, fixed organizational structure in the M-FORM.

    c. Importance of staff in "low" organizational levels and importance of dialogue between functions and groups in the N-FORM, rather than managing the interface in high management levels in the M-FORM.

    d. Wide organization communication in the N-FORM, instead of top-down communication in the M-FORM.

    e. A role of catalysts and architects of communication infrastructure, defined for the higher management, preserving the investment in knowledge in the N-FORM, rather than guiders, controllers, monitors and resource allocation definers in the M-FORM.

    f. A hierarchical organizational structure.

How do I protect my employees from confusion, inefficiency and organizational politics? I admit there is no full answer, but these challenges are addressed by assigning one (managerial) manager for each employee, to whom this employee reports regarding vacations and sickness, with whom s/he consults with when some high-level conflict rises, and with whom s/he speaks when they need to share their thoughts or feelings.

As with everything in life, there are no advantages without disadvantages. In order to help the suggested method actually work, good teamwork between the managers must exist. They must know how to cooperate; moreover, they must show good will. When good will is missing, the difficulties grow, and the advantages are not as promising.

When managers work in cooperation, everyone benefits. The employee benefits from improving development of knowledge and professionalism, as to the diversity in all dimensions described. The organization benefits with improved quality.

For the time being, I am an exception in this method of management. It is interesting to know how organizations will structure their knowledge-based units ten years from today.
Until then, let us wait with patience.

Yours,
    Moria

 Alon Zilberstein, 01/20/2009, 09:36
The description of the organizational structure reminds me of a project-based organizational structure.

Example from another organization,01/21/2009, 10:28
My partner's workplace has also taken this approach but unfortunately the workers experience mainly its disadvantages. The managers throw responsibility from one to the next and there is a blocking of mouths. Although there is one manager responsible for vacation and sick days, he has almost no power, so there he doesn't even try to help protect an employee who has a problem with other managers. The method creates much confusion and employees do not feel a sense of belonging to the organization, only to themselves. I'd be happy if you could specify what you think might help in this situation?

Moria, 01/23/2009, 07:40

Indeed the lack of good will, in the case described, has turned the method on its head, this being the reason that the brave commenter's husband experiences only the disadvantages. The specific solution in this case, to my understanding, is a clear definition of responsibilities and areas of authority. The organization is not ready, it seems, for the heterarchical model, which leaves ambiguity but also enables cracking this ambiguity.

A systemic solution will demand a change in the managers' labor relations. It is likely that the relationship described leads to many evils beyond this aspect of dumping responsibility on the employee. If the individual has the ability to influence and bring about change – great. If not, it may be better to wait for the right time to find a healthier organization in which to develop. Organizations have been more than a place to earn a living for a long time.

Anonymous,, 02/22/2009, 12:37

Organizations have been more than a place to earn a living for a long time. Can you expand on this a bit? And I am not referring to those who "live" at work, spending 14 hours a day in a workplace with a gym, swimming pool, resting rooms, dining room, etc., but an "ordinary" organization. What is the "more" from a workplace?

Moria, 03/04/2009, 05:47

An organization is more than a job: According to the Maslow's hierarchy of needs theory, we also seek in our workplace connections and belonging (Level 3), professional satisfaction (level 4) and personal fulfillment (Level 5). Incidentally these also have consequences that are not positive and form the basis of organizational politics. A workplace that only provides salary and employment security will not succeed in keeping knowledge workers for the long term, except of course in times of crisis.

2009-01-27 20:32

Employees leaving work

It is natural, in a blog dealing with management issues, to deal also with employees who leave. I admit that I always was too frightened to write a post on this. A live blog is not a book on the shelf. I knew that no matter when I would decide to write about employees that leave, the timing would be bad. Once, an employee decided to leave; another time, someone did not fit in and we announced that s/he should leave. Even if not all these situations are relevant, I run the risk, just by writing such a post, of putting existing employees under pressure, causing them to fear some unannounced plans.

Yet, I believe there is place for such a post in a blog that tries to examine all aspects of management. Therefore, I sat down and started writing.

There are three types of situations of employees leaving: There are employees who retire; there are employees who leave in order to work in another organization; and there are employees whom we decide to dismiss. An organization that nurtures a close relationship between itself and its employees hurts when the employees leave, no matter what the circumstances. An uncomfortable feeling exists among everyone: the employer, the leaving employee and all surrounding employees.

However, a, different emphasis should be placed in each of the three types of leaving employees:

When an employee retires, the main risk for the organization is loss of knowledge. An employee who retires has, in many cases, spent many years within the organization. In most cases the knowledge s/he has accumulated is unique and valuable. It is true that during this employee's work of many years with others in the organization, s/he had built relationships. However, regarding this coping, both the leaving employee and his/her colleagues have time to adjust. From the day we join an organization, we know that the day will come for us to retire. Nowadays, when people live longer and age later, many people wait for this opportunity of retirement and carefully plan their second life, after retirement. The emphasis, as already noted, is on knowledge retention. The organization has to prepare itself and manage a well ordered process: deciding what knowledge will be prioritized for retention; deciding what will be documented and how; deciding what will be accessible to all on an organizational website; deciding what will be transferred to other employees through conversations; deciding whether one employee will fill all job components, or if the role will be divided down and passed to several employees. Such a process should be managed. The responsibility of the leaving employee's direct manager includes: initializing the process, prioritizing what knowledge is to be kept, and more important, what knowledge can be dismissed (one can never pass on all knowledge). The manager has to decide who will take his/her place (one or more) and how soon the process should start before the employee leaves. And, when the knowledge transfer takes place, the manager needs to see that it actually happens at the right quality and pace.

We should not underestimate the complexity and importance of this process. We are speaking about employees who work in the organization for many years, and knowledge retention is not as simple as we wish. Knowledge transfer will not happen by itself. We must understand that even if we do everything possible, the expertise is lost and parts of the knowledge remain, The objective of a knowledge retention process is to retain as much as possible of the knowledge. In many cases, the manager is not sufficiently aware, and knowledge transfer takes place, but not at the right pace nor effectively. There are written methodologies on how to handle this issue, and I will not elaborate about the "how" other than say that it must be done.

When employees become consultants after they leave, they can, in many cases, earn more than before. Managers have to understand that this is not a healthy situation, as these employees tend to keep their knowledge to themselves in the years toward retirement. Our dependency increases in every generation.

There are employees who leave the organization at their own will. Changing careers and changing places of work is very common nowadays, Yet these moves make an uncomfortable situation for organizations. The employees that stay in the organization feel that maybe better opportunities await outside, and that maybe they are mistaken in staying. The managers find it hard to accept. I once had a manager who became insulted by every employee who decided to leave her. After she heard their decision to leave, she remembered mainly their faults - and we all have faults, even if we do a good job. Israel is a rather small country and, in such a market, people probably meet again at conferences, exhibitions, as suppliers or customers. In some cases, they even find themselves working together again in another place. Even if not, the manager has to know how to control his/her feelings even if they feel betrayed by the move. Business-like behavior and no expression of positive feelings are the best in this situation. Even if the employee left after the organization had won a new project that depended on this employee; even if there was an understanding with this employee about a planned promotion, which would leave others behind. Behave in a business-like way and express no bad feelings. Do not say any negative words, not even to the other managers. And of course not to other employees. A difficult task, but recommended.

In this situation, knowledge has to be transferred, but it usually is much easier than in cases of retirement.

The most difficult situation, as I see it, is when we as managers fire an employee. Sometimes this is a necessity, whether because of economic circumstances or because the employee is not the right person for the job. Certain issues should be addressed in this case:

First, we as managers must consider whether to enable the leaving employee to stay in the office after the announcement, or whether to disconnect him/her immediately, asking them to take their belongings and leave. The answer is complicated and varies from one situation to another. It depends if the employee works with customers and how the immediate leave-taking will influence the organization's connection with those customers; it depends how unique the knowledge of the employee is and how critical the knowledge retention process is. It depends on the risk of knowledge theft by the leaving employee; and it depends on whether immediate leaving will ease the departure or make it harder.

Another important issue to be addressed is how to prepare an employee for this traumatic situation.

There is no doubt that every dismissed employee experiences a trauma at some level. I was once dismissed, and I believe this a situation that I will never forget. Above the insult, work is our major source of income and stability. Without work, most employees cannot continue. When we hear such an announcement, we feel as if we are in an earthquake. What can I suggest as an employer? When possible, prepare the employee before. If the employee to be dismissed is someone less suitable for the job, speak about it a few times with the employee, urging him/her to improve and explaining implications of not improving. If they improve - everyone wins. Even if not, at least we partly prepared them for what was coming. I do admit that this is not as easy as it may sound. I find people have a hard time passing on this message. They try to be nice to the person and tend to soften the message, leaving the employee with a different understanding. The person on the receiving end may misunderstand the message even if things are said again, as it is not a pleasant message. I do not have solutions for all cases. I just think that passing on the message and preparing the employee for the announcement of his/her leaving is important. If I did not personally speak with the employee about leaving, I call to say good-bye and good luck. I find this behavior very important and helpful.

Another issue that comes up when we dismiss an employee is how to communicate the leaving to customers and suppliers. How do we communicate it to other employees? Also here, I must admit that there is no one simple answer, only one leading thought: we must be honest, while maintaining the employee's honor. It is important to communicate something true, yet retain respect. We can give part of the details, yet we must say something. Customers will understand.

It is important to communicate the announcement to all other employees almost immediately. I do this by writing an email at the end of the day on which the announcement took place: a formal, yet supportive email, speaking about the circumstances, and expressing my really sad feelings.
We must remember that what we do not communicate will be passed by rumors. It is also better if we pass the message and leave as little as we can in the open.
In rare situations, I have even spoken about the situation with groups of employees, taking advantage of existing staff meetings, enabling people to share their feelings. It all depends on the situation.

The last question on this issue concerns knowledge transfer. Most dismissed employees will not find it appealing to help the organization prevent the loss of knowledge and to transfer what they know. As this move is planned, part of the planning involves speaking with the direct managers of the employee at hand and deciding how to handle the critical knowledge, so that parts of it are shared even before the announcement takes place.

The issues are out there. They are not simple and I therefore find myself writing such a long post.
If I have to sum it up all in one sentence: knowledge to the organization; honor and sensitivity to the employee.

Yours,
    Moria

Natalie, 02/22/2009, 15:18

Hello Moria,

I have read a lot of your blog, because I am interested and I work in the field of knowledge management. As an employees who will shortly be leaving a job, the title of this post drew me in.

I am leaving my job for the second reason, and I really related to the issues you've raised about respecting and being sensitive to the person who chooses to leave.

An organization that can remember and remind the staff about the positive things the person did rather than the negative is a respectable organization, ethical and healthy organization.

And on the other hand, a person who can remember the positive about working in the organization is an ethical and healthy person. As you wrote, a lot of sensitivity is needed.

Thank you, I really identified with what you wrote, and was exposed to a new point of view.

Natalie

Anonymous, 02/07/2009, 3:40

Well this is indeed a very nice way to sum things up.

Improved living

2009-02-10 16:38

Diligence

Friday morning. Seven o'clock and I step into the supermarket near home. This is the opening hour, and within minutes I look around and the place is full. People arrive, fill their carts, say hello and goodbye and move on. Every time, this simple operation fills me with pride in the place in which I live. In Tel-Aviv for example, before ten o'clock in the morning, no one is up and about, certainly not in the supermarket. I always feel proud; we have diligent people.

Many people have spoken about the importance of diligence. Voltaire said that "The richness of a country depends on the amount of diligent people it holds;" Samuel Johnson claimed that "Few things are impossible to diligence and skill. Jean-Jacques Rousseau said that "Moderation and diligence are the true cure of the humanity," and in the Bible, in Proverbs, the Book of Wisdom, written by King Solomon, we find the saying: "Go to the ant, O sluggard, and consider her ways, and learn wisdom."

Diligence is ascribed to wisdom and success. Yet I have a feeling that this word, "diligence," sometimes has to be reminded, as we hear and use it less and less. I checked in Google and found the word mentioned only about 6 million times. Wisdom, in comparison, is mentioned 76 million times, success 435 million times, beauty 659 million times and love 2 billion times!

I can continue comparing diligence to many other words, but there is no need: the case is loud and clear. Diligence has lost its glory.

I believe that even though we are in the 21st century, it is very important that our employees are diligent and that we nurture them in this direction. Why? Because diligence is probably an essential component in good performance. There is, however, an additional reason: diligence is also an essential component in entrepreneurship and in an organization's ability to maintain itself not only in the present but also to step towards the future.

The interesting question is what diligence is on a practical level and how we achieve it. I will share my understanding of diligence and my way to achieving it.

There are several aspects to diligence:
First, a diligent employee works enough hours and tends not to miss hours or days of work. I speak with people whom I interview for work and explain that the work is at minimum nine hours a day. Many times, more is required. The truth is that I do not really require much more unless we experience peeks. Organizations that demand 11-12 hours a day do not deal, in my opinion, with diligence. I believe that this is more like taking advantage of people. Diligence is positive, yet our body and souls need rest so we can continue contributing also during the next day and week.

Another aspect of diligence has to do with the time in which we respond and act. Are missions delayed up to the last moment, or performed almost as they are given out? I have learned that missions that are performed rather early take me less time: we remember the setting and all related details and therefore save the energy of re- remembering all details. A diligent person starts early. In the Bible, we find people that started early. One example is Abraham, who got up early in order to fill God's request to sacrifice his son Isaac.

The last aspect regarding diligence, as I see it, has to do with the work we do. In every job, in every role, there are parts that are enriching, parts that challenge us intellectually and other parts we cherish less.. Sometimes we think a less skilled person could fill in; sometimes the work includes parts we do not like to do.
Even though it may be not the definition of diligence, I have discovered that diligent people never say no to a mission, also if they do not fantasize

about it. They never say they are overqualified or that they were not hired for this type of mission. Diligent people are prepared to work. Even if it is work and not fun.

How do I achieve diligence in my employees?
Two simple ways:

  a. I demand diligence from all employees, in all three aspects mentioned.
  b. I try to give them a good example by role modeling.

Does it work? I believe so. Even though we are in the 21st century and diligence is not a sexy or trendy word, the employees are diligent and I indeed appreciate them for that.

Yours,
    Moria

 Shmulik, 02/22/2009, 12:29

Hi Moria,
You have touched on a topic with which I identify strongly, and I would like to touch on another aspect of it. In many workplaces a culture has developed that causes the employee to be evaluated by the time he leaves from work and less by his functioning. According to this culture the most valued employees are those who stay late (though not necessarily working ...), no matter when they arrived or whether their time was used effectively. In contrast, workers who arrived early, worked diligently and went home "early" are valued less.

Recession

The whole world is now going through a difficult period. We all - in Israel where I live and write, as well as in the US and everywhere else - are experiencing a recession. Once, we used to think that globalization was a good thing. The recession has taught us that the absence of borders of place and time also has its deficiencies, and that globalization enables the spreading of less attractive factors from the US to China, Europe, Israel and actually every other place. Moreover, the US is not to blame. It can also start elsewhere.

How should one manage the organization in a recession period? How should one manage one's knowledge workers? Are there any guiding ru.les?
When one writes a book, one can choose to focus on specific areas, ignoring others, ignoring events. When one writes a blog, people expect you to be connected to reality and to existence. Not speaking about such issues may imply non-transparency and an unwillingness to open up.

Do not misunderstand me. The company that I manage, while writing these lines, continues to makes its living, continues not to lose. This, even though we all are already four months into an economic crisis. What will happen tomorrow? Will we continue to earn enough? No one can really know. For the time being, things are stable. Yet, this post is a necessity, as we are all part of something big, bigger than us. It is important to speak about this management issue, even though it is not easy to hear or to say.

As this blog deals with managing the employees, the post will focus on the relevant issues, leaving out economic or other business aspects, all critical to the situation.

It is important to express and show transparency at this time. This does not imply that every business detail should be announced widely, and that every time we feel bad after a customer shares distress with us, we should pass on our feelings, yet employees should be made aware about the overall situation and should be updated periodically, reflecting the changing trends.

I do believe that this transparency could be difficult to implement in times of growth and economic success. While experiencing a recession, this might seem easier to implement. Now employees are not willing to move to another place of work, as it is probably more risky to be in a place that you do not know than somewhere you already know and understand.

This, therefore, is not only a correct thing to say, but also an applicable one.

It is not less important to be sensitive to our subordinates. We must understand that each and every one of them experiences the instability differently, even though we are all in one company. The feelings may be a result of seniority in the organization, the job itself, the necessity as they sense it, and, of course, one's character.

It is important to be sensitive as each one of our employees has parents, husbands, wives and other close people who may be in distress or may even have lost employment. Such an event can affect the emotional and economic state of the employee.

It is important to economize and save. Be cautious! Too much saving can seem miserly, or drive a feeling of instability. It is important to show that now is not a party time, not a spending time. Nevertheless, some small spending is important for our souls and we must find the right balance in between.

It is important to share with the employees not only the facts regarding the recession and its impact, rather also regarding ways to change. Share with your employees and ask them to share responsibility in bringing in new customers. Sit and speak with your employees, asking them to come up with ideas how to offer more, or offer differently, considering the timing. This may result in better figures; moreover, we sense here the togetherness. People say that crisis is an opportunity. I would be happy to give up such opportunities if that's what it would take not to have any crisis. Yet, as the crisis is already here, let us drive higher cohesion between the company's employees.

It is important to be humble. To remember that even if we think we are the best, we probably are not, and surely are not perfect. Not everything is in our hands. In periods of growth and success, we as employers are captive somewhat, as we manage knowledge workers and these are free to leave and find some other place to work. Recession is an employers' era. We must not take advantage! We must remain humble. We must remember that tomorrow a different era might begin. Furthermore, we must remember to respect the other even though we are in charge and have the authority.

I read the lines above and suddenly realize; the crisis and the recession that followed teach us how to act, in times of crisis, but also in every other period. Maybe in a recession it is a necessity, but at all times it is probably the proper and more dignified way to act.

Transparency, sensitivity, cohesion, sharing and humility. Not too much - yet everything.

Yours,
    Moria

 Authority

Places of work are formal organizations: places in which authority is important and significant. In the mid 50's, when classic management theories developed, the source of authority was loud and clear: authority derived from organizational position. Every position had its status, and this granted authority. It was clear to each employee what was permitted and where boundaries were drawn.

Today, in the 21st century, terms of work have changed. The relation between the worker, and in particular the knowledge worker and his/her manager have become more complicated and less definite. Also today, we are not speaking about a symmetrical relationship, yet it is clear that the authority of managers is not as it was, and for sure does not derive from status and position alone.

Discussing authority includes two complementary aspects: discussing the source of authority and the delegation of authority.

Delegation of authority, or delegation of power, is not the same as transferring responsibility. When I delegate the authority to decide or act onto a subordinate manager or worker, they take on the operational responsibility, but the managerial responsibility remains mine. One can delegate authority permanently, temporarily, or as a one-time act; all these affect the responsibility of the employee. In all cases, however, the manager remains responsible.

Many managers find it difficult to delegate authority. In some cases, they literally do not pass any authority, which could be delegated, to make decisions or even to act. In other cases, they do, yet continue to ask questions and interfere, not giving up control.

The difficulty in delegating authority can derive from several reasons:

Sometimes, we start working on a mission that indeed is part of our job, but we continue on, even though it was correct to stop and pass the next stages on to one of our subordinates. This is the easier case, as awareness of this situation usually solves the problem.

Another reason has to do with the fact that we, as managers, are usually more senior, more experienced, and hence feel that if we complete the task by ourselves, not passing it to others, it will be completed faster and or maybe even better. I admit that from time to time, I also find myself in this situation.

A similar reason has to do with the energy we have to invest in explaining to someone else what we want to achieve, how and why, and in being sure that we get what we wanted. We feel that we prefer to complete the job by ourselves. In some cases, this may be the right solution, but the decision has to be made considering all aspects.

Sometimes, it is a task that we find more pleasant, and we wish to do it by ourselves.

In addition, sometimes, we are afraid. This has to do with delegation of authority being synonymous with delegation of power. This also has to do with the second part of this post, source of authority. We are afraid that if we delegate authority, we lose power and lose our source of authority. At the end of the day, we too, the managers, are human beings, and we wish to protect ourselves, whether consciously or unconsciously.

I can continue to add more reasons why delegation of authority is not as easy as one might expect. Yet this is not the main issue. The main issue is that delegation of authority is important.

It is important to reduce our burden and navigate our workload better;

It is important in order to develop the professionalism of our subordinates;

Moreover, it is important in order to build trust between us and our subordinates, and let them know that we are willing to trust them and rely on them.

A few tips to do with delegation of authority:

140

When you delegate authority, you must leave the employee who is in charge some free hand, both in freedom of choice and in freedom of action. Do not guide him/her down to the last point and leave them to follow only.

When you delegate authority, do not totally let go. Remember that some guidance is required, and some control is requested. Remember that responsibility stays in our hands.

When you delegate authority, communicate it in the organization. Also, to ease the operational level, but much more importantly, as a way of giving respect to the person in charge. Soft rewards are critical in motivating employees.

The discussion on authority is not complete without examining the sources of authority. As I already wrote above, the source of authority is changing as the concept of work and workers changes. In general, the source of authority depends significantly on the manager's knowledge. Employees respect managers who know. This, of course, is not the only parameter to keep in mind; employees will value a manager and accept his or her authority if they understand what is required, and if the request and demands correlate with the organization's values as well as with their own.

How do these influence managers and their behavior? I am not sure. However, in order to improve we all have to be aware of the changes in the source of authority. Moreover, we have to understand that authority delegation and knowledge sharing strengthen us and our subordinates.

Plato, who lived many years before we started working in formal organizations, spoke about authority, saying: "The wisest have the most authority." Those who are smart, who know, and have good judgment and keen discernment (definition of wise) are those who become a source of authority.

It took us many years and various organizational formats in order to go back to roots and deeply understand his saying. There are probably good reasons why this Greek philosopher, the student of Socrates, was one of the greater influences on our Western philosophy.

Seeing how wise he was, he certainly was a source of authority.

Yours,
   Moria

Marion Burgheimer, 22/03/2009, 17:59
Thanks for the interesting and honest post.
About authority and the delegation of authority I think that change in the attitude to authority and its delegation is culturally relative.
In more hierarchical companies the change in relation to authority will be narrower than in more equal companies.

2009-03-26 22:10

 # Rewarding

"Incentives and rewards are some of the most powerful management tools available." *Making innovation Work* (Davila, Epstein & Shelton).

People work for compensation. We do not expect people to come to work day after day and not receive anything in return. Yet, when we deal with rewarding, we redefine the scope, speaking not only about salary (or self-contentment in the case of volunteers). People expect to be rewarded; they expect a system that will encourage those who do well and punish those who do not.

A close examination of the above can teach about two objectives in rewarding:
The first sentence was cited from an excellent book I read on innovation. Innovation deals with changing the organization: leaving the current situation and replacing it by another one. Rewarding, according to the authors, is an essential tool for aiding this change and help transform it into organizational reality. If you want to change peoples' behavior, give them incentives before and while changing, and reward them after.
The second objective of rewarding is somewhat different. It deals with daily routine, motivating us to continually work and perform better. It resembles gasoline, of which every car needs a steady supply in order to continue driving. This need is part of our human genetic make-up, and it only grows with us being knowledge workers, choosing whether to stay and how well to perform.

It is obvious why rewarding is so important: to help maintain and to help change.
The problem starts when rewarding is not as simple as we might wish.
It is not simple to reward, since, says the research, too much rewarding leads to poor performance. I think the reason is twofold: first, people get used to the rewards, and the level of rewarding required grows higher.

The second reason has to do with the fact that people understand that less is required from them in order to actually win the reward, and they will naturally tend to make fewer efforts.

It is not simple to reward since no company lives in a vacuum: the employees have expectations regarding what they were used to in previous work places, in relation to what they hear from friends and family, and in relation to what happens in the market in which the company operates. It is all too easy to be drawn after others and build a rewarding system that does not serve us as a specific organization. If we act otherwise and do not answer employees' expectations, dissatisfaction and de-moralization can follow.

It is not simple to reward, as rewarding should be proportional to the phenomenon or behavior that we want to encourage. As I have already written in previous posts, measuring is difficult. In many cases, it is complicated to estimate how much each individual contributed to a certain success.

The main question, however, is not why rewarding is not simple, but how it should be done.

First, an organization has to conduct its own rewarding system, based on its unique organizational culture. I recommend not following others, not being drawn after the industry, neighbors or friends. The saying "we are unique" can lead to a positive implementation, if communicated properly. Of course, expectations should be leveled with new employees, before they are hired, and as part of the interviewing process. In the case of an existing organization that wishes to change its current rewarding system, things are more complicated. I read a study, conducted by Kaplan, claiming that people tend to become fixated on existing incentive and rewarding systems and resist the change. Such a change has to be managed, according to all well-known change management methodologies.

Second, any rewarding system has to be based both on organizational needs as well as on individual needs. In general, organizational needs are in high congruence with achievements and results, while individual needs are more connected to efforts. Both need to be rewarded. Rewarding can be "hard," namely money in all formats: higher salary, bonuses, stock options, etc. Rewarding can be "soft," with examples including recognition, promotion, publication, compliments, professional course, etc. Using Maslow's needs pyramid can help in designing the reward system. What I find important is to balance between the two, being sensitive and wise.

Any rewarding system, no matter its design, should answer some principles in order to be effective:

- Fairness. Creating a situation where other employees understand why their colleague was rewarded and not them. Any rewarding system should aspire to reward individuals when the organization was rewarded significantly.
- Answering the individuals' needs. Whether the rewarding is for a team or for the individual, s/he has to be touched and motivated.
- Balanced in scope. Too generous rewarding systems are not considered effective and in some cases harm. Too little yet communicated rewarding will cause cynical interpretations.
- Flexible. Never pre-define everything. There are always are unexpected situations in which an employee should be rewarded. The rewarding system has to be flexible enough to answer these situations as well.
- Stable. Do not change the rewarding system too often.
- And most importantly-
- Suitable. Fitting the organization's spirit.

I hope we all succeed in rewarding our employees and motivating them to work properly and change when appropriate. At the end of the day, we have to remember that rewarding is one of the most powerful management tools available.

Yours,
   Moria

Marion Burgheimer, 04/23/2009, 12:12

It is important to me just to add that in rewarding culture has a great influence. There are some societies that are individualistic, such as the USA, where personal reward will be far more acceptable than in collectivist societies such as Italy and South America, where the tendency to reward the work group would be greater.

Christian, 04/03/2009, 2:29

Many years ago, in a large public sector organization where I was to introduce knowledge management, I was told that it would be impossible to change the culture. Indeed, people were keeping their knowledge to themselves, believing it was their power and survival. In the end, rather than running a large change management initiative, we decided to change only a small little thing: the annual performance review would include a section rewarding knowledge sharing behavior.
Generally speaking, you cannot change the culture, but you can create the environment for the culture change to happen.

2009-04-08 14:18

Electronic mail

The Israeli Defense Force (I.D.F.) has announced that it is presently working on a new rule that will limit email sending so that any soldier can send an email to another soldier only if he or she is up to two ranks higher than him/herself.

There is no doubt that electronic mail has influenced our lives and has influenced management. This example of the new army rule is one example that demonstrates how much technology influences culture and the flattening of the hierarchical organization structure.

Is this something good? And if not, is it right to block it? Maybe, in the 21st century it is rather a good idea to flatten the organization or at least reduce the mental gap between the organizational ranks.

The issue is complicated; however, no matter what the final decision is, I think that two things have to be considered in the decision-making process:

a. Technology should not dictate culture. Each organization has to analyze the possible advantages of organizational flattening, and potentially there are indeed advantages: the employee thinks more broadly, looking at the big picture, as the organization does not treat him as a small part in a well-defined organization. Also, good new ideas can be better diffused. Furthermore, here in Israel, many people know one another from several different life cycles, having different hierarchal relationships in each; etc. If these advantages are greater than the disadvantages of emails to all (I will not elaborate on the disadvantages as we were all brought up on them and know them), then we should favor free email usage. Of course, if this is the case, new boundaries should be set, preserving the manager's place as the final decision maker.

b. If it is decided to make a change, like the one reported to be in I.D.F., then the change has to be managed. It should be communicated, explained, and not only commanded from above.

147

The reason is obvious: employees already became used to this ability. Any change will be interpreted as a worsening of conditions and can cause bitterness. The move and its rationale should be communicated, and special care has to be dedicated to the interim period while people become used to the new work process.

However, email usage has more in to it for the 21st century worker, beyond organizational flattening.

Email has totally changed our availability to work. Even though we all have cellular telephones, people do not tend to call us after working hours (and yes – the definition of working hours is tricky). With emails, we have no problem. We can write whenever convenient to us, and if it is not work time, we assume that the employee, receiving the mail will answer when s/he finds it suitable. Without noticing, we reach a situation in which most of us work, write to each other, exchange opinions and tasks almost 24 hours a day.

Emails have also changed our routines during working hours. Sometimes we have the feeling that email is managing us, rather than us managing it. It seems as if every half an hour the mail carrier arrives, with a new big sack filled with mail, leaves it on our doorstep and goes off to bring the next one. The piles grow higher, and the small message on our inbox notifying us how many mails yet have to be read and/or handled leaves us stressed, hopeless or both. Some people reach a situation in which they reply to mails all day, and again, somehow the mail is the initiator managing us, and we are the responders.

What can I recommend? I manage the time in which I answer mails. Emails are treated mainly during evenings, nights and in the early hours of the day. Most of the daytime hours are dedicated to people. I do enjoy the advantages of email without letting it gain control over me (at least most of the time).

A post on emails cannot end without discussing the email's content, beyond the framing (to whom and when). Email is somewhat risky. On the one hand, we regard it as less formal, like speaking on the phone, or even speaking face-to-face. We speak unofficially and therefore do not always consider every word we use. Email, however, is written. If we get an email from a colleague, or even worse, a subordinate, and are under the impression that they hurt our feelings, we read it again and again, empowering the insult. It is very different from a situation of face to face speech. When speaking face-to-face, and even on the phone, the one with whom we are communicating can sense our feelings. S/he can fix the impression, clarify things, apologize, or limit the harm. With emails we do not have this luxury: on the one hand, they are informal; on the other hand, very formal.

What is recommended? To read every mail we write and consider if there is any chance it will be misunderstood; to use the email channel to shorten processes, but use it on positive issues; to remember that a third person can pass and see what was written. The bottom line: do not give up this fabulous channel, yet use it a bit less than what would seem natural.

Email indeed is a revolution, a revolution of the 21st century. A technological revolution that has influenced quality of life, pace, and the ways we treat our managers. I do think that at the end of the day it does have more advantages than disadvantages, and we should be happy with it.

And, yes, I think that organizations can be flattened, at least in most cases (of course, I do not know what is best for the army). Authority in the 21st century starts from knowledge and is less influenced by formal hierarchies. The manager has to invest more to be appreciated and treated with honor; this is much about the ability to send or not to send him or her an email. The knowledge era builds its own balances between things.

I wish us all benefit from the email revolution. I wish we will have many other positive revolutions.

Yours,
    Moria

 Ronit Nechemia, 04/22/2009, 7:06

Hello Moria,

I agree with your words thoroughly. Indeed we have become slaves of email. Or at least I have. I open my mail almost 10 times a day and devote much time to answering emails. I will try to adopt your idea of limiting response time to certain hours.

On the subject of flattening organizations, indeed email helps, because it is now easier to contact people levels above you to talk about activities, etc. Unfortunately, though, there are still organizations that have not implemented work with e-mail, making it difficult for day to day functioning and lengthening response time. And here I come full circle to my opening sentence.

Be Well

Ronit

Avi Zucker, 04/22/09, 15:26

Agreed - e-mail is a revolution, or more correctly - another step in the huge media revolution we have been experiencing in the past decade.

As a work tool we want to use it wisely, each in his own way and according to his needs – just like pen and paper, mobile phone, or landline.

I'm not sure email is a dominant factor in flattening of organizational hierarchy. It also goes through secretarial filtering in many places.

It could be that we tend to attribute some of the ills of society or an organization to revolutions and changes, and place the responsibility for these on the on the most comfortable and prominent cause – but this is not always the true cause.

In antiquity it was often the case that cruel rulers would kill the messenger baring bad news. Could it be that e-mail emphasizes and reflects processes taking place anyway? I hope that regulations, orders and procedures for email use will not lead in that direction.

And of course I join your hope for many more positive revolutions

Marion Burgheimer, 04/23/2009, 12:02

Good post.

You touch on an important point related to time. But sometimes people also ask whether the other side will look when the mail was sent and what he would think if he saw that it was sent on a Saturday or at odd hours of the night.

In some cultures, "extra work" in relation to hours can be viewed as strange or unbalanced.

Regarding the writing style for emails - I agree. I also think that sometimes people forget that is it still a dimension of writing; emails sometimes end up looking like oral conversation without opening, transition and closing words.

Teamwork

We live in the 21st century. If we examine the people around us and ourselves too, we notice something that was different in the past century: individualism. People in life and employees at work, all seem to be very individualistic. One may say that this is almost a religion. Oscar Wilde, in his book *The Portrait of Dorian Gray*, expressed this in his unique way: "being in harmony with oneself is a key to life, echoing the tenet to Aestheticism that calls for the individual to make of his own life a work of art."

Individualism conflicts with teamwork. The willingness of one to placate oneself, to achieve self utilization, to succeed in building a career opposes the need to fit yourself to your environment, to people who may work and think at a different pace and who may
have other perceptions and other agendas.

Thinking in terms of the organization, there seems to be a conflict as well: we were taught that teamwork is a good thing. However, teamwork costs more: more time for synchronization and more money since duplication exists.

Yet teamwork should not be considered part of the past. Teamwork is a value, one of the values that belongs not only to the Human Resources department, which seeks the ideal. Furthermore, in the 21st century, when many of us are knowledge workers, and our knowledge is one of the main factors driving the organization's success, teamwork is important or even essential, threefold: from the individual, the organizational and the business perspective.

I shall explain:

152

Even though as individuals we may yearn for individualism, we need a network of support and a sense of belonging. These of course can be developed on an organizational level, with no teams, but are not enough as such. We need a close group of reference. One that will see us in the morning and ask why we seem worried. One that will share our happiness and success and our sad moments as well. One that we can turn to when we are in distress. A close group. Belonging can be built also within big groups; however, being part of a team conceptualizes the belonging and makes it feel real.

In past years, a new type of relationship has emerged, similar to teams, but actually serving some other functionality: social networks. A social network deals with relations between people, but focuses on weak relations whereas in teams we deal with tight relations. A social network cannot be a replacement and solution that provides the level of belonging or the support network provided by a team structure.

On the organizational level, teamwork is a very important value. In their book, *Collaboration 2.0*, Levine and Coleman write that teamwork includes, among other benefits, the following advantages:

a. It strengthens the individual's commitment;
b. It raises the satisfaction level from the workplace;
c. It enables advanced trust and communication.

No doubt, obtaining even only one of these is enough for us to understand that, organizationally speaking, teamwork is a positive thing. All the more so when speaking about all three.

Professionally speaking, teamwork is surprising. We might have thought that in an era of knowledge, when everyone has his or her own expertise, there is no real business benefit to working in teams. However, this is not the case. Teamwork brings better business value than working separately. Nonaka and Takeuchi, in their book T*he Knowledge Creating Company*, taught us how Japanese companies create the dynamics of innovation. Knowledge, they write, develops in teams / small groups and not in the individual experts' brains. Socialization is what they call the first stage of four in which knowledge is created. This stage deals with transferring the tacit knowledge from the individual to a close group. The knowledge may start from the individual, but it develops through the transition and within the group. Other researchers, who analyzed learning processes, agree with this finding: Teamwork improves the quality of products and other outcomes, improves the efficiency of obtaining them, and advances the innovation and creativity related to them.

Teamwork brings improvement to the individual, to the organization and to the business.

Nevertheless, so I believe, life is not as simple as it sounds. Working in a team is not always convenient. People have to compromise and understand that the team may work or decide according to their colleague's recommendations rather than to theirs.
Teamwork can cause a herd effect, where the group influences the individual and not always in a positive way.
Moreover, teamwork can yield duplication in the cost of resources.

How can the potential of a team be utilized? Buchel, in her article "Knowledge Creation and Transfer: From Teams to the Whole Organization," published as part of Nonaka's and Ichujo's book *Knowledge Creation and Management*, writes about two main factors of the team, influencing the human capital and improved performance:
a. Density of relations within the group.
b. Bridges to the outside (organization, stakeholders, etc.)

How can a company avoid the duplication challenge? I think that the solution to this problem lies in defining clear limits: defining the tasks where teamwork is advantageous, and those better performed by one individual. Analyzing, brainstorming and interviewing are examples where teamwork should be preferred, even if it may seem to create duplication. Implementation, technical operations and documentation are examples in which teamwork may be unnecessary and even a waste of time and money.

One last point, before ending this post. I started with individualism. Individualism has many benefits, and it must not be sacrificed in the name of teamwork. Combining both, teamwork with place for the individual and his or her uniqueness, is a key to success. As Michael Jordan said: "talent wins games; teamwork and intelligence win championships."

Yours,
    Moria

Nick, 04/26/2009, 3:35

.. Nice post, Moira - thank you.

My only comment would be to question whether the individualism you recognize is at least partly a cultural factor. It is certainly there in the US and (to a lesser extent) in the UK, and I assume from your post that it is there in Israel also. In Scandinavia and in the Far East, I would say it is far less of a factor.

Also, I would like to add, as a support to the teams (assuming they are multidisciplinary teams) the cross-team networks and communities. This adds a third dimension - the individual, the team, the community.

Ram Bansal, 05/03/2009, 6:23
Since individuals are the building blocks of a team, individualism remains valuable in team work. But every relationship puts some tab over liberties of the individual, which is not felt by the individual if he/she is socially disciplined.

But conflict arises between individuality and team-spirit if the two have different value systems. Today, with degraded human values all around, even the most disciplined feel suffocated in a team.

156

2009-05-11 10:51

 # The physical work environment

In his book *Thinking for a Living*, which deals with how to achieve better performance by knowledge workers, Prof. Tom Davenport dedicates a whole chapter to the issue of the knowledge worker's physical work environment.

When I think about an invested work environment, the first example that pops to mind is Google's offices. The slides, the fire chutes (enabling one to descend quickly) and the various games and entertainment areas, all leave me with the impression of a place with fun. The massage booths (with professional masseuses), as well as the relaxation areas (armchairs and aquariums), enable rest to any employee also during formal working hours. And the list of other perks is long.

Fifteen years ago, I worked for a short period in a start-up company. If there is one thing that I won't forget from there, it is for sure the kitchen. The kitchen in this place was always full. The refrigerator always seemed to be overloaded, having every type of delicacy one could dream of. The closets were always filled up and twice a day someone in charge came in to refill. People arrived to work very early as breakfast seemed much more appealing there than at home. People left later, staying for dinner at work and, of course, discussing work at the time. I always thought that this is a cheap and easy way for the organization to see that its workers work more and produce more: give them the right conditions and they shall stay more and produce more.

The interesting question is what influences the performance of the knowledge worker in terms of physical work environment? How is it right to organize the workplace?

In the mid nineties, as Knowledge Management emerged as an independent discipline, some organizations invested in building special complexes nurturing knowledge sharing and development. It became

157

popular to invest in many cozy coffee corners, encouraging the employees to speak more one with another. The assumption that led to this was that when an employee encounters a problem and does not solve it by himself immediately, he will take a coffee break, where he/she will meet a colleague and discuss the issue. There is a good chance that the conversation can help, whether because the colleague has a good idea, or whether because the employee has spoken about it and found a way to progress. Coffee areas became part of the trend of organizational Knowledge Management efforts, enabling informal knowledge sharing.

Another phenomenon that developed over these years, also present nowadays, is the design of special areas for knowledge development. Skandia, for example established its future center accordingly, back in 1996.

Do plants and lighting encourage thinking? Are colors like red, blue and yellow better for creativity? And, maybe, whiteboards across the office walls (with markers nearby, of course), enabling one to write down every new idea as it pops, are the key to successful knowledge development.

Davenport, in his book mentioned before, has researched this issue of the physical work environment. His conclusion is that even though many companies have acted in several ways in order to provide a more efficient workplace, very little can be said for certain as to the effects of the workplace on the knowledge worker's performance. Davenport claims that the attitude towards this issue should be about two aspects of fit: customized and personalized:

Customized - fitting the physical work environment to the group and its knowledge needs, based on the fact that knowledge workers should be segmented into sub-groups, each having its typical workplace needs.

Personalized - as knowledge workers like the autonomy of deciding for themselves, if possible, choice has to be granted to them as to their workplace.

A new trend that I have heard about in several big high-tech organizations has to do with setting up virtual workplaces. The supporting rationale is that the today's employees are mobile employees: they come in to the office only part of the work days; they have mobile telephones and laptops, and a fixed workplace is not really needed. Instead, virtual work-stations are populated every day with the employees who need them on that specific day. This solution can also be used if people do not have laptops or mobile telephones. Technology enables one to connect to every computer and login to his or her environment using their User ID and password, and connect to their fixed number just dialing some instructions on the phone.

No doubt that this solution can save any organization a great deal in the short term. Rent is expensive and should not be ignored. This solution is one among a series of possible solutions, from which any organization has to pick:

a. A private room for each employee.
b. Team rooms.
c. Open space (a cubicle for each employee).
d. A virtual workplace.

In order to understand how the environment influences the performance of the knowledge workers, I believe three factors should be considered, each affecting the performance, whether directly or indirectly:

- The ability of the workers to concentrate and promote their tasks.
- The workers' ability to share with one another.
- The workers' satisfaction from work, as affected by the physical environment.

If we analyze all alternatives, we see that there is no one correct answer:
Private rooms may enable optimal concentration and may be most satisfactory, as a private room refelcts the employee's status, but they enable less sharing.
Team rooms enable sharing but may decrease concentration;
Open spaces give a bit from each;
And virtual workplaces are cheap.

I favor team rooms (3-4 people in a room). Assuming knowledge develops in teams and groups (as Nonaka suggests) and that fellowship/ friendship / team spirit develops with togetherness, I think this is the best solution performance wise. I know that concentration can be negatively affected, but there are several ways to handle this challenge:

First, remember that it is rare that all employees are together on the same day in the office. Knowledge workers, as already stated, are mobile and spend a lot of hours away from the office.

Furthermore, those with laptops can always wander to other rooms in order to hold a noisy telephone call (and not interrupt others) or in order to work on some task where they need silence (and not to be interrupted by others). The organization has to verify that such rooms exist, and that such a move is legitimate.

Also a request to work at home in order to promote such a task should be treated favorably.

And, last but not least, when people work in a joint room, they develop a culture of considering one another.

What else do we need?

No matter what you decide to do, I have one wish: do not promote a virtual work environment in your organizations, even if it has financial benefits. Understand the importance of a private corner, a place for personal pictures, a plant and some nonsense on the table. They are all part of the worker, and even though it may not be proved by research to improve performance, it is surely important for the employee's feeling and sense of convenience and comfort. At the end of the day, we invest much in order to give our employees a feeling of belonging, so why spoil this?

Yours,
Moria

Nick, 05/11/2009, 9:55
Nice one Moria.

Avigdor, 05/22/2009, 16:51
Hello Moria,
This week I enjoyed reading the two articles you wrote in your blog: "Managing in an era of knowledge." I always read the new articles published on the blog. This time, I particularly enjoyed reading the articles on work environment and teamwork, and I really identified with what you wrote, which fits my world view well, and was well and fluently written.

Employees' commitment

A famous joke tells of a pig and a chicken walking together and discussing the possibility of opening a restaurant. "What shall we name the restaurant?" asks the pig. "Simple," answers the chicken. "We'll call it 'Bacon and Eggs'." "I am not sure about this idea," says the pig. "It's true that we are partners, but while you are involved in the business, I am committed."

What is commitment and how should we create organizational commitment? These are the questions I would like to explore in this post.

Thinking of organizational commitment brings to mind issues of job satisfaction, feeling part of the organization and similar concepts. All these are related to commitment, but are not identical. Organizational commitment is a psychological engagement of the employee to the organization.

Why should an organization work towards such commitment? There are several reasons.

First, commitment improves employee retention. We invest so much in knowledge workers; we spend many hours nourishing and deepening their knowledge. An employee that leaves forces us to re-invest. Furthermore, we depend on many of our employees. In some organizations, employees have strong relations with customers, making the personnel change unpleasant to the customers; in many organizations employees hold invaluable information, which will be lost if they leave. If employee commitment to the organization reduces turnaround, we should no doubt encourage such commitment.

We could settle for this reason, but apparently there are other benefits to an employee that is committed to the organization.

162

A committed worker is more productive during his working hours; a committed worker, according to studies, works more hours and performs better. A committed worker is less absent, identifies with the organization and better assists in meeting its goals (see Dr Sigal Weisner's PhD thesis on the importance of an individual's commitment)

In order to understand how to achieve employee commitment, it's important to understand the different types of commitment.

Commitment can be characterized by several dimensions: one deals with the nature of the commitment: an emotional commitment versus a beneficial commitment (the benefits of staying within the organization) versus a moral commitment.

Commitment can also be viewed from the perspective of motives: intellectual motives affecting commitment, like a high chance of not finding an alternative job or the comforts of the current job, versus emotional motives affecting this commitment, whether positive (liking the people we work with) or negative (fearing the need to get used to a new job).

Yet another aspect is the object of commitment: an employee might be committed to the profession and thus (partly) to the organization; or an employee might be committed to people in the organization, either to top management, direct management, colleagues or customers; some employees are committed to the organization itself, seeing themselves as part of it and wishing for its success.

We can also refer to the scope of commitment: interpersonal or organizational. On the personal level, research has found that older people are more committed than youngsters, women more than men, laymen more than educated professionals. We also see personal character as an influential parameter of commitment.

The organization and its organizational culture play a major role: a culture of sharing, teamwork and participation in decision making enhances employee commitment.

The <u>professional</u> aspect has great influence on the level of commitment: clarity of job description , volume of activity and personal ability to develop all affect commitment level.

If I had to choose one parameter affecting commitment, just one tool, I'd choose reciprocity: be committed as a manager to your employees and to their wellbeing. The rest will follow.

Yours,
    Moria

2009-06-10 06:58

Setting an example

"Practice what you preach" is a common saying.

In the twentieth century, people worked all their lives in the same place. You could have hated your manager; you could have considered him/her a tyrant or a lazy slob. You could have attributed any negative characteristics to your manager. None of these were reason enough to leave your workplace. Some would even say that these were the roots of employee common culture .

I would not say that everyone today loves his or her manager. Nevertheless, a manager's behavior is important, very important. It is claimed that people join organizations for the promise of an interesting job, but they leave because of managers. We expect, and rightly so, that our managers will set an example for us to follow. As managers, it is important for us to set such an example.

How to set an example and in which areas?

An organization is a complex system, and it takes different people working together to create the engine that drives it forward. Even in my line of work (managing a consulting firm) I soon learned that employees with different expertise are required in order to enable progress. The conclusion of all this is that setting an example is different from expecting everyone to duplicate your actions or your results. Such an imitation is not necessarily the correct way to set a positive example.

So what needs to be done? In a post I wrote about measurements, I presented an idea that is suitable for this side of the equation as well, for setting an example: measure values as you measure results, I wrote. Values represent the strategy by which we wish to act. If those are correct, and people are following them, we are on the right path.

The same can be said about setting an example. I think the key to a good example is values and hard work. It is important that we set an example by getting results, but the lesson to be learned is the road to those results rather than the results themselves. We set an example by demonstrating correct values.

I try to work a lot. I believe that luck and talent are components of success but that hard work is no less important. I work in the early hours of the morning and I work at night. I find time to rest but my work takes most of my time, even on weekends. I don't expect my employees to work as hard, but it is important for me to set such an example.

I follow our company values. I try to project professionalism, innovation, humanity and collaboration in my actions. I admit it is not always easy. I am, for example, an individualist by nature, and it took me years (actually, it is taking me years; I haven't completed the mission yet) to learn how to share. I put a lot of effort into it. I do it not only because it is right to share but also because it important to set an example. As I wrote in the beginning, to practice what I preach .

There is another aspect of setting an example. David, King of Israel, committed one of the most horrible sins: He took another man's wife and then had her husband abandoned to his death on the battlefield. We could have asked why God gave us such an imperfect king. Why didn't we get a perfect king, one whose example would be easy to follow?

Those who think King David is not a positive example misread the Bible. Ours is a complex world and nobody can be perfect. Giving us a perfect king, or writing only of his good qualities, would set too high standards, standards that we would find hard to relate to. If this were the case, we would have no standard at all because of the major gap, because of the notion that we can never be as perfect, so why bother?

A manager setting an example can and should expose his/her weaknesses as well. We do not have to be proud of our shortcomings, but we should not hide them. We all make mistakes. All of us, as employees, even the most professional ones, occasionally make wrong decisions. Setting a positive example includes, in my opinion, exposing the less positive aspects as well. It is not that we are proud of these aspects. We are not happy with them. It's just that, like King David who sinned and repented, we admit our mistakes and try to learn from them. This is a positive example in my mind.

It is also important that we remember, as managers and as parents, that setting an example does not always result in your employees or children following your exact footsteps. Remember that values are the important issue. If we plot the correct values, and set an example by following those values, there is a good chance that our employees, even if their professional decisions differ from ours, will follow our example .

And as Albert Einstein said: "Setting an example is not the main means of influencing another, it is the only means."

.

Setting an example is important. We should do so.

Yours,

   Moria

Courses as a training tool

Woody Allen is quoted as saying "I took a speed reading course and read *'War and Peace'* in twenty minutes. It involves Russia." This joke, apart from being just funny, reveals a lot of skepticism about the value of courses as a learning mechanism.

It is clear to all of us that we need training in every line of work. When we hire new employees, we must not assume that they have the knowledge sufficient to perform their duties. There are two reasons for this:

The first has to do with the organization and its environment. Even if the knowledge worker held a similar position in a different organization, we must assume that in our organization the job will have different characteristics and will require different skills.

The second is continuity. Knowledge related jobs evolve over time. Training is required in order to continue to meet tomorrow's knowledge challenges.

But, as Woody Allan hinted, there are two main challenges related to courses:

The first is unrealistically high expectations. We expect to read *War and Peace* in twenty minutes; we expect students to be more skilled coming out of courses.

The second is the question of answering a real need. Is speed reading the requirement or is it the assimilation of new knowledge? Are we sending our employees to have their minds filled with procedures, while forgetting the essence?

I would like to concentrate on the first challenge of this post: not on the topics of training but on the methods used to achieve effective training. How can we touch each and every student, ensure that they absorb, understand and assimilate the training material, and improve the chance that they will have better performance as they come back to the organization. After all, this is the purpose of all training, as Peter Jarvis defined as early as 1958: "Learning is an improvement in performance when the stimulation, the situation and the motivation remains unchanged."

I'll start by saying that courses are complementary tools for training, learning and knowledge management. If sharing and developing knowledge, the building blocks of knowledge management, are daily events, then courses are the peaks whose aim is to boost employees' knowledge and performance.

How can we achieve effective training through courses? I think the key lies in understanding the four learning styles defined by David Kolb:

   a.   Concrete experience – A chemistry teacher illustrating an idea by a lab experiment.

   b.   Active Experimentation – An athlete improving his performance through many running practices.

   c.   Abstract conceptualization – Reading an article on prisoners' rehabilitation.

   d.   Reflective Observation – Listening to a case study analysis of a certain organization.

It is interesting to note that we, as humans, learn through a combination of the four styles. Even more interesting is the fact that some of us prefer certain styles and find those easier to learn by. In other words, the mix of learning styles is individual.

What can we learn from this?

Let's go back to the course and its instructor. It is reasonable that this instructor prepared the course combining his/her preferred learning style, preferred teaching style and understanding of management expectation from the course.

It might be that these three are actually one style.

If we want effective training, we must demand that instructors equally combine the four training styles in their lessons. They must acknowledge that the students in the class have different learning styles.

And on a practical note:

training by abstract conceptualization - in explaining concepts and grand ideas;

training by concrete experience - going into details and explaining how these details implement the grand idea;

training by reflective observation - including a lot of stories and case studies in the training;

and lastly - training by active experimentation as much as possible.

Seemingly, this is nothing new. I attended a training conference this week and heard there that we should change from lectures to active "hands on" experience (Active Experimentation). It was said that this could be proved by looking at babies who learn by doing, not by sitting in the classroom.

No friends! Do not follow this or any other trend. It is not wise to choose one style and rule out the others. Combine. And remember that each one of the students has a different learning style, and we need to create the best combination, one that will enable every student to match his/her personality.

In this way, I believe we can improve students' understanding and produce effective training aimed at meaningful learning. I do not believe we will read *War and Peace* in twenty minutes following a speed reading course. I do believe we will read it faster than before and we are sure to remember more than it involving Russia...

Yours
   Moria

Silence

I was invited last week to give a lecture at the Israeli accountant's annual convention. This presentation was unique in its length – I had to present for two hours continuously. At a certain point during the lecture I felt that I was not using my voice properly, so I started pausing between sentences. Suddenly I understood the obvious: there are advantages to these pauses, other than relief to a sore throat. I tried again and noticed that people were paying more attention. Silence echoes the spoken words and gives the audience time to understand. I was reminded of my childhood swimming lessons. The instructor showed us four motions. The last one was a "no-motion," relaxing the body before the next set of motions. This had the same effect as silence.

Silence is a human and management tool. It amplifies the other's attention to our words, and improves their understanding. Silence, however, can serve other objectives as well.

When we are on the defensive, we prefer to keep silent. If we are not sure of our deeds, silence will prevent further complications. This is not always an adequate tool and should be used with care, only when appropriate in a broad perspective, and not just from short-term considerations .

Silence enables listening to other people. Not only hearing, actually listening. If we are really silent, not just keeping our lips still, we can concentrate and listen to what is being said and more than that – how it is being said: what is the body language saying, what is not being said and why.

It is interesting to note that silence is an alternative to shouting. Roaring silence is heard in the distance.

What I find most fascinating is not the power in silence, nor the scream it replaces. It is ability of silence to get others to act that makes it such a special tool .

It is claimed that sales people use this tool too. When they feel the deal is close, and the customer hesitates, they will take out the contract, mark a small 'x' where a signature is required, turn the paper to the customer, and silently wait. It's hard to believe, but most people will sign at this stage.

This technique can be used in other circumstances as well. By being silent, we invite the other side to act. Human nature makes it difficult (at least for most of us) not to react to silence, so everyone will try to act when the other is silent. The beauty of this tool is in its simplicity.

As managers, we must consider employees' silence. When an employee is expected to speak and keeps silent, what can we deduce?

First, all the above is true about employees as well. The employee might be using silence as an alternative to shouting, as a way to better listen or be heard, or as an attempt to move us into action.

Nevertheless, we must consider other options as well. When an employee does not answer, he may have misunderstood what was said and be too embarrassed to ask. We must analyze the silence and, if this is the reason, try a different explanation.

It might be that the employee disagrees with us and is reluctant to argue. I am not saying we should encourage employee resistance, but we must be aware of this option and assess the situation to decide whether to accept this silence or try and break it.

And maybe they just had nothing to say and we are speculating too much…

Communication is 20% verbal and 80% non–verbal (body language, intonation etc.). In silence, we don't have even that first 20%.

We must try harder. But if we listen, there is a chance we will understand. When people are silent, they are saying a lot.

Silence is a powerful management tool and we must learn to use it more. I am finishing now.

It is time for silence.

Yours
  Moria

Anita Santiago, 07/21/2009, 12:09

Very interesting perspective. I've never thought about using silence as a tool. You're right, we generally are silent when we are defensive. Your article gives great examples and I will to add this to my 'toolkit.'

Empathy

How many times have you gotten so mad at someone that you wanted to burst, shout and tell the other person exactly what you think of him/her, but managed to hold back? It happens to me and I guess it happens to everyone else as well.

The thing is that the anger remains after we hold back. Many times it is still there and even if we settle down a bit, the problem was not really solved.

As adults and as managers we know that sometimes you just can't say everything to the other party. Sometimes you have to wait for the right moment and, in some business circumstances, that moment might never come.

The challenge is in channeling anger and other emotions born out of disagreement to a productive place. The challenge is calming down.

Empathy is the ability to identify others' emotions and share them. Empathy is not sympathy. Sympathy deals with the emotional side of identifying others' hurt or joy. Empathy is the cognitive ability to understand and be aware of the emotions the other is going through and, as a result, to sympathize. Empathy can help us in several ways:

First, by understanding our employees, customers and others, we become more relaxed and less angry. It helps us see the whole picture, and sometimes recognize that ours is not the only just perspective. Even if we are certain of our position, understanding the other side weakens negative sentiments.

174

Second, by understanding we can improve our performance: if you understand why a potential customer is hesitant about acquiring a service, it will be easier to get into a conversation and offer a better solution, thus increasing the chances of you becoming a preferred service provider. If you understand your subordinates, it will be easier for you to care for them, to avoid some crises and better handle others..

Understanding, when used properly and not as a manipulative tool, improves our morality.   The organization gains, but, first and foremost, we gain.

How can we be more empathic?

I will start by saying that empathy is a personal innate characteristic. Studies show that some babies are empathic to other babies' (non-hunger related) cries. (See Hoffman's studies on the subject). Empathy can be seen to exist, on some level, in other mammals as well. However, it is also important to note that empathy can be acquired.

The first step is intent. We must really want to understand the other in order to succeed.

Other people, like us, are motivated by needs and values. If we are to understand their meaning, we must come up with several alternatives to needs and values that drive their actions / decisions / behavior. Analysis of these alternatives will bring us closer to understanding.

The last step has to do with our actions. After we understand what others are going through, we must decide on the right management tool and the ethical course of action. It is not always about canceling our previous decisions, but maybe adjusting the way we implement them, the tools that accompany them and yes, sometimes even changing the bottom line .

We must remember: empathy is a cognitive process, but it involves emotion.

And, unlike many other situations, when one applies empathy there are no losers. Empathy is a win-win situation.

So let's be more empathic and gain.

Yours
   Moria

Marion, 08/24/2009, 11:46

Good post. The linkage between the explanation and the business/ organizational/ management ideas is important. Thanks a lot!

2009-08-06 16:11

 # Winning

Life is never only routine. It is full of wins and losses. Winning is usually related to competition against somebody else. Winning is related to zero-sum games; I win, therefore somebody lost. This is different to success, which is not relative to somebody else but focuses on the achievement.

The first association that comes to mind when thinking about winning is wars. The Six Day War win (1967); the Hasmonian win that Jews celebrate on Hanukah (a 2000 year old victory); the American win in the Gulf War etc.

The concept of winning, however, is not foreign to organizational and business life. You can win a bid for a new contract and you can win a business lawsuit. Usually in the everyday life of organizations you win a debate.

Debating is natural. It is natural that different people will have different interests, different perceptions and, sometimes, only a different reality interpretation that leads to different conclusions.

The thing is that when we debate, whether with a customer, an employee, a colleague or a new applicant, we sometimes digress from debating and decision making into a competition that ends with some people feeling that they "won" while others feel they have "lost".

Naturally, I love winning, both as a person and as a manager. If there is a win-lose situation, I'd rather be on the winning side.

2,000 years ago the term "Pyrrhic Victory" was coined – meaning a victory that is actually a defeat. Pyrhus was king of Epirus who won the 279BC Asculum war against the Romans (thanks to Wikipedia). When congratulated for his achievement, Pyrhus said: "one more such victory would utterly undo me." This reply was due to the loss of most of his army and some of his best friends and senior officers in the battle. I think that today, in the 21th century, some of the victories we experience against those closest to us – customers, employees and colleagues – have a lot of loss in them.

Why? Every time we achieve something, and somebody else feels that he lost because of our achievement, then in fact we lost as well. The other person is bitter, maybe angry, and his pride might be hurt. Going back to military jargon, we can say that we won the battle but lost the war.

What do I suggest? In no way should we chose an "always give up" policy. It is contrary to human nature and is a bad business approach besides. It is nice to suggest a "win-win" strategy, but this is not always practical. Hereby are a number of tips:

First, try to balance. Give up sometimes, if the loss is not too expensive, in order to give the other person a good feeling.

Second, look for "gray" solutions. Furthermore, even when the answers are very clear, you can, and sometimes should, create ambiguity and gray shades in the way you communicate these answers.

We must not forget, however, that sometimes the bottom line is important and sometimes we want to put the other person in his right place, even if s/he ends up feeling as if s/he has lost. In those situations, it is vital that we are aware and willing to pay the price of the other's "loss."

Do not brag, in any case, no matter what. Remember this is zero-sum game and bragging can cause bad feelings in the other.

One last tip: "Winning is a dangerous intoxication" (Achad Ha'am). Take care.

Yours
    Moria

Val Patrick, 19/08/2009, 11:48

Winning is one aspect that everybody wants...but the greatest winning moments are when you fail or lose and you are still standing and learned from your defeat... You used your experience in order for you to win...

Negotiation

I must admit that there are many things that I enjoy doing as a manager, yet negotiation is not one of them. The term always reminds me of some unpleasant past occurrences.

Do not misunderstand me; I know how to negotiate. Sometimes I benefit; sometimes I lose. As in other issues in life, we experience both. However, knowing that I have to negotiate does make me happy.

Negotiation is a process we have carried on for thousands of years, from the early days of history. We tend to relate it to commerce, but actually almost every discussion between two people or groups, no matter the issue, includes some negotiation.

As this blog deals with managing people, I wish to examine the issue of negotiation through the perspective of negotiating with employees.

The first negotiation with the employee that we handle as managers occurs even before s/he starts to work; we negotiate with the potential employee regarding his/her salary and terms. As I believe that negotiation leads to negative associations, not only to me, rather to many people, I also believe negotiating with the future employee not to be such a good idea:

If I refuse the employee his/her requests, even for the correct reasons, the employee can go for years with the feeling that s/he has lost.

If I accede, wishing to start the relationship with the best possible feeling, people will hear and know, and I will find it more difficult to insist on what I think is right in the future.

Even if after negotiation we compromise and reach an agreement, the employee may always remain uncertain, thinking that if s/he only argued more, or maybe used other tactics, things would have ended differently.

As I have been in the working world for several decades already, not always running a business of my own, I can say that as an employee, I think I experienced all three scenarios...
Coming back to the starting point: good it is not.

What is the alternative? I try to reduce, as much as possible, situations of negotiation with employees. Negotiation outside the organization is possible, sometimes even a must, but inside the organization less is better; less times; less powerful.

How do I manage?

With potential employees, with such a sensitive issue sensitive (salary), and at such a sensitive time (trust not yet having been established), I avoid negotiation completely. I listen to the employee, and evaluate his/her abilities, knowledge and experience in comparison to existing employees in the organization, offering a fair salary, as I understand, relative to the others. Working this way, I benefit twice: once with the potential new employee, preventing the negotiation; in addition, towards all other employees, who know that someone else does not earn more than they do just because s/he argued better.
Do I also lose? Of course I do. It is naïve to think otherwise.

However, this is only one process in the lifetime of many processes and many situations. As much as I may wish to avoid negotiation at all, I know it is both wrong and impossible. Every person has his/her opinions, interests and ways in which s/he understands life. Negotiation is necessary.

A few tips I use when negotiating:

First, I remind myself that negotiation is a process of trade: give and take. If I entered a negotiation, obviously, I will have to give something. I think in advance what I am willing to give and where I put my limits.

I manage the negotiation openly and fairly. Openly – by sharing with the person in the negotiation, in early stages of the conversation, where I am willing to concede. Fairly, by suggesting limits that I think are fair (and I know I am subjective) and unbiased, even if I have an advantage.

I know that I am willing to pay for results. Doing this is not as simple as it may sound, but it puts me in a better position. If I leave the manager-employee relationship for a minute, a good example demonstrating this is negotiating a working contract with a potential customer. I start the negotiation, knowing my red lines, knowing they are fair for both sides, and knowing that if I lose the contract because the other side insists on moving the line, it is OK with me. I do not work if the price is not reasonable.

I listen to the other side, trying to have a professional, yet pleasant and calm conversation. Much research has been conducted, teaching that handling negotiations with positive feelings may only help. We know this is true. Nevertheless, there are situations in life where conversation turns vocal. On some occasions, this happens without control, in other situations, as a way to impress and confer a message. No matter why this happens, it is important to bring the conversation back to a positive atmosphere and as soon as possible.

And always, but always, I try not to take the anger too far in any negotiation. If I seem angry, if I feel angry, I always remember the positive things I know regarding the person I am negotiating with, and try to return to a baseline positive atmosphere.

I also know that negotiation is the bridge to agreement. Therefore, it is not as horrible as it may seem.

Yours,
    Moria

2009-09-09 18:10

 # Vacation

Last week I took three days off. Three full days (or maybe two plus) on which I did no work. I was on vacation.

Maybe some of us have not noticed, but in the past few years, as technology has developed, the lines between work and home are not as sharp and bright as they used to be. If in the past people worked constant hours, today the situation is quite different:
Many people have personal computers belonging to their workplace. They connect after formal working hours from home. Others connect through their personal computers, answering emails and helping in other urgent matters. Even banking and defense-based companies, which cannot reach their materials outside the organization due to security, find themselves answering phone calls at various hours (we all have cellular phones nowadays). Those who work in global companies, or with global connections, experience never- ending working hours as routine.

Vacation, therefore, is the only time when the worker absolutely rests from work. There are organizations which consider weekends as full rest, but I have seen many organizations, where people partly work on weekends. Some, belonging to homeland security, others, preparing proposals towards deadlines. Furthermore, weekends are too short for people to really rest and stop thinking about work. Most of us continue to think about work every weekend, even if we do not actually work.

It is important therefore that we, the managers, see to it that our employees take vacations. It is important that we also take vacations ourselves. Of course, it may seem that for the organization, it may be more profitable that employees work more, and we pay them for the vacation days.

Intensiveness of work in this knowledge era and also working during non working hours make this need for vacations so essential.

Some tips I can share from my experience as a manager:
Firstly, I never enable my employees to amass vacation days, not using them within the ongoing work year. Those who do not go on vacations will erode over time. In some rare cases, the manager even has to force some employees to take a vacation. This should be done if necessary.

Three days are the minimum for declaring a real vacation.
Furthermore, it is recommended to separate between vacation and errands days. Taking off three days, but using half of them for errands, is not a good idea, and does not help the employee really freshen up and rest. Enable your employees to be flexible, and from time to time, settle their errands on working days, enabling them to work on non-standard hours. Enable the employees to sometimes work from home, allowing them to get service and repairs from home while working. Try encourage the employees to take vacations "serving their soul." Of course, not all vacation can serve as such, but try ensure that at least one vacation every year is for fun and rest.

Above all these, and please forgive me parents of children that do not agree with me, remember that vacations with children can be enjoyable, important and positive, but are not equivalent to personal vacations or vacations with our partners. A parent, taking two weeks vacation on August, is not a person that rested and truly took vacation. He or she just worked somewhere else. Try encourage your employees, if possible, to take at least one vacation a year without their children. And my dear children, if any of you are reading this, please know: I love you so much, despite what I wrote.

In between, treat your employees with equanimity. Once every few months, enable them to start late in order to have a good breakfast with a friend, or leave early in order to go out and see a movie. Not exactly a vacation, rather a mini-mini one.

And again, do not forget to look after yourselves as well.

Yours,
  Moria

 Mike Petersell, 09/23/2009, 7:02
You make a good point about vacation being the only time a person can truly refresh. I have three employees and they are all remote workers. They work hard and they have a difficult time separating work from their home life. Being away on vacation is the only time they can truly refresh.

I encourage them not to stockpile vacation days, but they do like to save a few for the end of the year during the holiday season.

Mike

Excellence

I know of no organization that does not list excellence as one of its core values.

Everyone wants success, each organization according to its mission and goals. Ask any employee, from the senior manager to the junior employees, what excellence is and they will know what you mean. Some can articulate their understanding while others are less clear about it. However, everyone understands excellence.

I will take some of that back. It is said that "perfect is the enemy of good." This saying implies that too much investment in quality could be wrong: it might do more harm than good; it might have only marginal benefits and, in other cases, it might not be cost effective.

We must refine the definition of excellence to include more than quality: product quality, service quality etc. We must include cost (money and other resources), and define excellence as the combined success of all these elements.

The million dollar (or maybe more...) question is: "What creates excellence?" How do we implement this marvelous value? How do we create an excellent organization, where excellence is employees' goal and they manage to achieve it?

I recently read a book about excellence called: *Outliers: The Story of Success,* written in 2008 by Malcolm Gladwell. I discussed the book with my daughter, who read it as well, and she highlighted an interesting point: the book talks about our tendency to attribute success and excellence mainly to talent. It shows, one example after another, how other factors, unrelated to talent, are the makers of success. I tried to learn from the different examples what to do as an individual and as a manager in the 21st century, who has stated (yes, me too) excellence as one of the four core values of my firm. My daughter pointed out the pessimism in this book: it gives a lot of credit to opportunity and cultural heritage in achieving excellence. These two factors are driven by chance, not by brains. This is indeed a pessimistic approach. But, despite this direction, opportunity and heritage hide many other parameters that influence success: hard work, patience, education, discipline, meaning (see also *A Whole New Mind* by Daniel Pink), communication etc. I counted a long list of about 15 elements that affect success and excellence.

I do not believe in long lists. I believe in Pareto and in our need, as individuals and as managers, to focus on the top three elements. I tried to compile my own excellence factors list. Three was not enough but I managed to stop at four:

Professionalism. A combination of talent, education and experience.

Hunger. Never being satisfied with what you have, ever wanting more.

Meaning. The knowledge that a mission is important, that it will give me satisfaction (Maslow's hierarchy of needs).

Teamwork. Collaborating with people of different backgrounds and complementary experience. Simply – working with other people.

The first and last factors are those I can influence as a manager. Assigning meaning to our work can be done at a top level, even if it is not easy on a day-to-day basis. Creating hunger is not easy at all. We can role model, set challenging goals, but here our influence is limited.

I almost forgot – positive feedback. Complimenting people for their effort and success are always factors that motivate them to try and succeed next time.

To sum up, let us look at a different point of view, proposed by Marva Colllins (in *Spirit of Aristotle*): "Excellence is not an act but a habit. The things you do the most are the things you do the best".

An excellent day to you all.

Yours,
　Moria

Shlomo Kiznur, 10/22/2007

The parameter of "hunger" is, in my opinion, very important. As the son of a Holocaust survivor, "hunger" sometimes sounds inappropriate. Still, I think the world of plenty in which our children are being brought up together with the lack of "hunger" for challenges and actions to achieve what our parents could not in the early years of the state (because their situation was different from ours, not because of any lack of talent) have caused a decrease in striving for excellence in the country's youth.

2009-10-07 15:47

 # Flexibility

Kyuzo Mifune is one of Judo's experts (after Jigoro Kano, Judo's founder). When asked about Judo's essence, Mifune said: "Judo rests on flexible action of mind and body. The word flexible however never means weakness but something more like adaptability and open-mindedness."

As in many other management topics, we can learn about flexibility from the art of Judo. I think an organization that offers flexibility to its employees has a great advantage. In fact, it seems to me to be one of the important aspects of working in an organization. An employee who has experienced a flexible organization will have a hard time in a more rigid workplace.

In this post, part of a blog about managing employees, I'll concentrate on flexibility toward our subordinates. There are other aspects of organization flexibility. An organization that easily adjusts to market trends, for example, will succeed. But, as I stated, this is not the subject of this blog, and I will focus on flexibility in managing employees.

Why is flexibility important?

Operational flexibility makes employees' lives easier. It reduces vacation time spent on everyday chores, and increases effective work time even if the employee is a parent to little kids and has to leave work early. Even more so, operational flexibility enables employee evolution. It helps managers answer different employee ambitions, as well as their unique needs as employees and human beings. The result is improved organizational achievement as well as better employee development. Most importantly, flexibility leads to better employee satisfaction, and this in itself is part of their promotion.

How can flexibility be applied?

Operational flexibility can mean flexibility in the place of work (such as part time work from home); the time of work (night time, morning hours); flexibility in authorizing special expenses (such as return of money when receipts were lost); flexibility in using vacation days and allowing leave without pay, etc.

Managerial flexibility can mean flexibility in the level of control over each employee; flexibility in the training program assigned to each employee; flexibility in employees' career building path; flexibility in job description. The list is endless.

Every organization needs to be flexible according to its abilities. There are some areas where a larger organization can be more flexible, such as defining many education programs and allowing employees to choose between them. In other areas, small organizations find it easier to be flexible, since the chain of command is shorter and the bureaucracy can be reduced. This means that there are no winners and losers. Every manager in every organization must understand the potential for flexibility and exploit it as best they can.

Where must we refrain from flexibility?

As in any other aspect, too much flexibility can damage. I try to put three limits to flexibility:

Don't be flexible when there is a chance the law will be broken (reporting work hours for a public organization);

Don't be flexible as an excuse for giving up on principles;

And don't be flexible when it can be interpreted as favoring some employees at the expense of others that were not treated in a flexible manner.

How do you know when to be flexible and how not to cross the line? I don't have a concrete answer. Who said life was easy?

Above all, flexibility implies that we trust our employees. Do not worry: even if some will abuse this trust, most will repay our trust and flexibility in kind.

It is worth it.

Yours,
   Moria

 Nick Milton, 10/11/2009, 1:02

This interesting post made me think about the concept of flexibility in dance.

To dance with a partner, you need to be flexible and responsive. However flexibility is not the same as floppiness or looseness - you can't dance with someone who has floppy or loose arms (dancers call it "spaghetti arms") because then you lose connection and you lose linkage.

Instead you need what dancers call "frame." Frame is caused by a degree of tension in the arms, that allows you to sense, to feel, to connect, and to react to your partner.

Flexibility in the partnership between an organization and an employee is good, provided it is within a frame; a framework of trust, but also a framework of boundaries. You talk about the rules and the law - there need to be clear boundaries - a clear frame - to the flexibility.

Flexibility also needs connection, for without connection, there can be no response and no flexibility - just looseness.

Flexible, connected, within a framework.

So, thank you for an interesting train of thought!

Leadership

Close your eyes and think about leadership. What comes to mind is the term charisma and names like Ben-Gurion, Winston Churchill, Martin Luther King, Jeff Walsh, Rudy Giuliani, Lee Kuan Yew and many others. Something beyond reach; not people like us. We are people and perhaps managers; they are leaders.

Peter Drucker, in his book, *Managing for the Future: The 1990s and Beyond* (1992), discusses the importance of leadership to organizations. James Surowiecki, in his book *The Wisdom of Crowds* (2004), reached the same conclusion. Managers, he claims, transformed during the nineties into leaders or even superstars. Think about the list of names above, and what became of those people. Most managers failed in other organizations, after leaving the one where they excelled. Political managers were not re-elected or ended their lives in solitude.

Reading the Drucker book reveals that despite his book is known to speak about leadership, it is actually about economics, people, products, marketing, managing and organizations. In the few pages dealing with leadership as we know it, Drucker writes about lack of managers' charisma and about charisma as a curse for managers.

Heifetz and Linsky wrote an interesting book about leadership *(Leadership on the Line: Staying Alive Through the Dangers of Leading*, 2002) and, like Drucker, shatter the leadership myth. What is leadership? It is the activity of leading a group through change.

As I write this, I feel this post is different. I quote a lot of others, instead of talking about myself. And, indeed, compared to giants like Drucker and others, I am humbled.

Am I a leader? If we accept Drucker, Hefez and Vlinsky and remove charisma, then I can say I am a leader, a change leader. I lead change in the perception of knowledge management in Israel, and of its professional implementation. I am not alone in this process, but I have done my share:

in developing methodology, teaching it through seminars, articles, newspapers and portals, and by actually implementing it in many organizations.

I lead my firm. I move it forward to success and to stay in the lead.

In other areas I am not a leader. I am satisfied with what I have.

Of all the things I have read and learned about leadership, I find the following to be most important:

Firstly, the understanding that leadership involves sharing. Despite the "lone ranger" impression of the leader, lack of emotional and practical support will make change management very difficult; it makes leading people harder..

This item is first for a reason. It is not trivial and I don't want to create the impression I wrote it just because it is "the right thing to say." If we fail to understand that we are part of a partnership, we lose twice: we will fail in business and it will be easier to fall into the pit of arrogance.

Belief in the cause is also important. Leaders lead significant changes - if the change was simple, it would have happened by itself. The leader must have faith, willingness and motivation. Belief in the cause, belief in the way, belief in his own willingness to lead the change and in his ability to do so.

It is important to understand that leading change is not a "9 to 5" day job. Leading change requires total 24/ 7 dedication. We must be willing to invest all of our time and energy into the organization and the change we are leading. It has a price tag. The price is spare time, quality family time. There are no free lunches, and we must be aware of that.

It is important to know proper change leading methodologies. We won't get into details. I wrote a specific post on this, and even there could not fully cover the topic. Some people have good intuition and can lead change without proper study, but for most of us, success in leading change can be improved by learning.

Last, but not least, setting an example is important. We must set an example of hard work, proper conduct; we must set an example by implementing what we require of others. Leaders who fail to exercise their own teachings will not have long-term followers. As Lincoln said "You can't fool all the people all the time (in all matters)".

In the Bible we read about different leaders. It is interesting to see some negative details about the great leaders, even though the Bible is sparse in details. The best example is David - a great king, conqueror and believer. Alongside these characteristics, the Bible tells of his improper behavior towards Bathsheba. Some scholars try to explain David's behavior, and insist that he did not sin. I prefer others who say he erred and sinned. I think the Bible tried to show leaders as flesh and blood, capable of mistakes, in order to make it easier for us, so that we understand that leaders are not far from us. We can be leaders as well, even if we have our faults. Each of us managers can be a leader. We must want this. We must be determined and not despair in spite of resistance (and there will be resistance). We must be wise in our leadership.

We must be 21st century managers.

Yours,
    Moria

2009-11-11 05:50

 # Epilogue

I have been through twenty years of management and two years of writing this blog. I am not giving up management, but I think this blog ought to be closed. Most topics have already been covered and additional posts are bound to repeat existing ones.

Am I the ideal manager? Obviously not. Do I make mistakes? Sometimes. Even when I follow the path outlined in this blog. I know that real life is more complicated. There are issues that not be covered by any post; Different values, contradicting each other, can be covered by different posts, but in real life they have to be faced together and the dilemma has to be resolved. There are times that I stick to what I planned, but being only part of the situation (even if it is the manager's part), I cannot control others' behavior in having things done my way.

 Does this imply that my observations are impractical and do not yield results? Not at all.
They improved my performance and I think that, at the end of the day, they contributed to my success.

I hope that reading these ideas, adding them to you own experience, and implementing them in real life scenarios will assist you as well.
I can say for myself that developing these ideas over the years, testing them and even formulating them for this blog, has done and is still doing a great deal for me.

I thank you for reading this blog and for the encouraging replies I received. During these past two years of blogging, besides the written talkbacks, I received additional support in other forms.

Thank you.

Yours,
    Moria

p.s. I may return with another blog. Goodbye for now.

www.ingramcontent.com/pod-product-compliance
Lightning Source LLC
LaVergne TN
LVHW022314060326
832902LV00020B/3452